IT'S A
BITTER
LITTLE
WORLD

WRITER'S DIGEST BOOKS
Cincinnati, Ohio
www.writersdigest.com

IT'S A
BITTER
LITTLE
WORLD

THE SMARTEST
TOUGHEST
NASTIEST
QUOTES FROM
FILM NOIR

CHARLES PAPPAS

Visit our Web site at www.writersdigest.com for information on more resources for writers.

To receive a free weekly e-mail newsletter delivering tips and updates about writing and about Writer's Digest products, register directly at our Web site at http://newsletters.fwpublications.com.

09 08 07 06 05   5 4 3 2 1

Library of Congress Cataloging-in-Publication Data

It's a bitter little world : the smartest, toughest, nastiest quotes from film noir / by Charles Pappas.

    p. cm.

 Includes index.

 ISBN 1-58297-387-3 (pbk. : alk. paper)

1. Motion pictures--Quotations, maxims, etc. 2. Film noir. I. Title: It is a bitter little world. II. Pappas, Charles.

  PN1994.9.I87 2005

  791.43'6552--dc22

                     2005013417

Edited by Kelly Nickell
Designed by Claudean Wheeler
Production coordinated by Robin Richie

F+W PUBLICATIONS, INC.

Dedication

Dedications are for pussies. "To Snookums." "To my one and only." "For Fruit Cup." Whenever I read them I start choking like this one time I got a chunk of cheese popcorn caught in my throat. They're always the same Cinnabon of schmaltz, an FTD bouquet of wuv, a big fat Hallmark card with "Raindrops on roses and whiskers on kittens." The spouses/lovers/significant others/ICM agents they're dedicated to? I'd bet like Pete Rose on opening day that they'll be playing whack-a-mole on each other in divorce court or "Page Six" of the *New York Post* before the book's remaindered. Who am I going to "I heart [ ]" anyway, my two ex-wives, especially numero uno, a dead ringer for Linda Fiorentino in *The Last Seduction*? Or Lynn, the Delilah who turned out to be Phyllis Dietrichson in *Double Indemnity* only with Jimi Hendrix's wardrobe, and a taste for Patsy Cline, gin-and-tonics, a cult that bought noir-heavy Raymond (Perry Mason) Burr's Pacific island, and more lies than an Enron balance sheet? She graduated summa cum maraud from *The Killing*'s Sherry Peatty's finishing school for female biohazards. Like death-destined Johnny Clay told Sherry after she gives him a look you'd wrap a thong around: "You'd sell out your own mother for a piece of fudge." Sherry sold out her husband George like a nag at the Elmer's Glue factory. George was played by Elisha Cook, Jr., who sad-sacked his way through 120-plus movies, including vintage noirs *Phantom Lady*, *Born to Kill*, and *The Maltese Falcon*. Cook was the Elvis of losers, the Dom Perignon of the doomed-his suits were funeral shrouds draped over his crow-bait frame and his eyes bugged out like a scuba diver who ran out of oxygen. Noir without losers of Cook's caliber would be the Louvre without the Mona Lisa, the sheep without the bleat, the redneck without the mullet. Because you were the chum for the shark, the Yugo on the highway of life, the gazelle chased down by the lion on *Mutual of Omaha's Wild Kingdom*, Elisha, this book's for you.

About the Author

Charles Pappas traced missing heirs and tracked down the last wills of the rich and famous. *It's a Bitter Little World* is the first in a projected series on noir and popular culture. He lives in La Crosse, Wisconsin, with a dog who eats bees and has a daughter who's always right. He can be reached at chassoho@aol.com.

CHAPTER FOUR
The Money and the Grubbing

CHAPTER FIVE
The Life Lessons and the Death Wishes

CHAPTER SIX
The Quotes That Dreams Are Made Of

APPENDIX
The Best and the Bleakest

INDEX

The saga of Orpheus and Eurydice was the original noir. Even at his wedding, Orpheus, the lyre player, was as doomed as Walter Huff the insurance salesman in *Double Indemnity*.

The god Hymen showed up to bless the nuptials, but his smoking torch cast a shadow blacker than anything in *The Big Combo*.

After Eurydice died from a snake bite, Orpheus followed her like a faithful little dog into the underworld the way Dave Bannion did in *The Big Heat*. Bannion had a gun; Orpheus had a lyre. Nothing stopped him from bringing back his Eurydice. But in the end, his need doomed her and killed him. Just like *Chinatown*. Instead of sirens like Evelyn Mulwray, Orpheus was tempted by Thracian babes. And when they couldn't seduce him, they ripped his head off like the pull-tab on a can of Miller Lite and threw it in the water. In love, in life, in noir, that's as good as it gets.

I Was Tussling With the Most Dangerous Animal in the World, a Woman

My first Eurydice was a six-foot-tall shot of espresso. She was from Somalia, back when the Soviets were *The Man Behind the Curtain* there. She had cheek bones that only existed in the mythical lands of *Vogue* and *Elle*. Big, round Monet eyes. She followed me around and borrowed books from me she never read. One night I sat cross-legged on her shag carpet floor, while she sprawled on a couch with so many cigarette burns it look liked the Marlboro Man himself had used it for target practice. She told me the story of her life from that couch. It took her just eighteen sentences.

"I'm already married," she said, "but it's no big deal. I married him so I could stay in this country. I thought you should know."

"Where is he?" I said. I was seeing the door fly off the hinges, a *Deliverance* hillbilly pushing a shotgun though my teeth and shooting me Old Yeller-style, yards of yellow crime scene tape around my Hamburger Helper remains.

"I don't know." She looked like I had just asked her how to translate "pre-mediated murder" into Somali. "He's in the army somewhere."

"I also have a kid," she said. "It's in Somalia. I had it so I could get out of my parents' house. I think they still have it." Now she made one of those Mr. Yuck face stickers you see on bottles of poison.

"What about the father?" I asked.

"He was a dissident. He plotted against the government. I got tired of him, always complaining. Complaining, complaining, complaining."

"What happened to him?" The take-out Chinese food we had eaten before was twisting in my gut like larval worms.

"I wanted to get out of there. I mean, Somalia, you know? I turned him into the KGB and our secret police. They gave me money for him so I could leave the country and come here."

I felt like I had just discovered the insect parts they really make my hotdog from. Then she poured the whipped cream on top of the gravy and tossed a cherry on top.

"Does that make me a bad person?" she said. The cheekbones turned into switchblades. Those long legs I wanted to get my Ph.D. in now looked as inviting as a pair of bat wings. I never saw her after that night. But I've been chasing her all my life.

INTRODUCTION

The dreamer never challenges the reality of a good dream while he sleeps; but he will tear and claw his way out of a nightmare. Maybe that's why film noir never had one pat definition, like the Western did. It's always been a nightmare, in the words of Eddie Muller, author of *Dark City: The Lost World of Film Noir*, of "seemingly innocent people tortured by paranoia and ass-kicked by Fate."

The term *film noir* itself means "black film." The French film critic Nino Frank minted it in 1946. He was riffing on the first use of *noir*—describing the British Gothic novel—and *Série Noire*, the name for translated American hard-boiled detective fiction by authors like James M. Cain, Raymond Chandler, and Dashiell Hammett. Being French, the critics and their minions later put film noir on a pedestal and sneered at anyone who disagreed with their de facto definition: Film noir had to be shot in black and white. It had to have run between 1941 to 1958. It had to be urban. It had to show the scratched B side of postwar accentuate-the-positive America. It had to start with *The Maltese Falcon*, and it had to end with *Touch of Evil*.

But film noir was much more than a type of cinematography or an it-started-here-it-stopped-there era. Its underworld ambiance came out of the classic American gun ballets, like *Little Caesar*. Its offbeat camera angles (which take the point of view of a drunk on the floor trying to stand up, or a near-death out-of-body experience) were fathered by German expressionist movies such as *The Cabinet of Dr. Caligari*. Its classics were made by German directors who fled Hitler, including Fritz Lang (*The Big Heat*), Billy Wilder (*Double Indemnity*), and Robert Siodmak (*The Killers*).

Its darkness was more a matter of cheap lighting than artistic choice. Its streets were greasy with rain and its buildings were *Nighthawks* lonely. Its meals were cigarette smoke and stale coffee. Its women had jewelers' loupes for brains and cash registers for hearts, and they stomped on men like they were the peanut shells on the floor of a rotgut bar. Its men were loners and losers, war veterans, and amnesiacs with more blank spots than a book of Mad Libs, men who were—sometimes literally—trying to find out who they were. Its criminal bosses had a fetish for violence, like burning victims' ears with cigarette lighters, torturing them with a hearing aid, or beating their partners to death with a pair of bronzed baby shoes, like Jack Webb does to his *Dragnet* sidekick Harry Morgan in *Appointment With Danger*. Its voiceovers were the sermons of emotional zombies.

Its authority figures' grip on credibility was thinner than Gypsy Rose Lee's G-string. Its shadows loomed like black ghosts haunting the living. Its background music was a trumpet or a saxophone as sad and frantic as the wailing of a trapped wild animal gnawing its foot off. And the love of men and women wore off quicker than the booze or the perfume.

True noir changes with the hemlines, the TV shows, and the *Billboard* top ten. It Toyota'd out of the city and into the desert (*U Turn, Red Rock West*), zipped up a down jacket and mushed north (*Fargo*), rewound into the past (*Miller's Crossing, Chinatown, The Two Jakes, L.A. Confidential*), fast-forwarded into the future (*Blade Runner*), microscoped *The Joy of Sex* cover to cover (*Body Heat*), and crammed the CliffNotes for French deconstructionists (*The Usual Suspects, Memento*). Its piano-key colors are now beetle blacks, lab-coat whites, gargoyle grays, tobacco-stain browns, and autopsy reds.

Whatever its latitude and longitude and shade, noir will always be Greek tragedy. In Aeschylus's *Oresteia* (a letter bomb containing *Agamemnon, The Libation Bearers*, and *The Eumenides*), fate deals out harsh destinies that are as undeserved as those of the victims of a tsunami. In noir, as in tragedy, there are more ironic yet inevitable endings than in O. Henry and *The Twilight Zone* put together. Good and evil are Siamese twins, the victim is sometimes as guilty as the victimizers, the point of view is often the criminal's, and his temperament is the same as his fate. In noir, the worst and most powerful people in your life know all your secrets and all your lies and ultimately must use them against you. No matter how good the plan or how noble the intention, in noir there is always a snake in paradise, a worm in the apple, a monkey in the wrench.

In noir, they chase the stuff that dreams of money are made of (*The Maltese Falcon*), or stubby boxes of radioactive material (*Kiss Me Deadly*) or containers with a mystical glow (*Pulp Fiction*). But it always comes down to this: In noir, what you need gets you killed.

The Origins of Noir

In the beginning there was the word, and it came out of the mouths of babes named Velma. Or mugs like Chuckles or Dix or Verbal. They weren't plain-melba-toast, Jello-mold, PG-rated, barbershop quartet, malt-shop, white-picket-fence, Wonder-bread-with-mayonnaise, "Honey, I'm home," in-separate-beds-by-ten-o'clock words, either. They were the words of film noir— *The Big Heat, The Asphalt Jungle, The Big Clock, Double Indemnity, The Big Combo, White Heat, The Usual Suspects, The Big Steal, Blue Velvet, The Big Carnival, The Big Knife, The Big Sleep, The Big Lebowski.* So many of them have *big* in their titles because they use bulked-up, big-mongous words that bruise like King Kong on crack ...

> **MR. WHITE:** You shoot me in a dream, you'd better wake up and apologize.
> —*Reservoir Dogs*

... break bones like nun-chucks ...

> **TAXI PASSENGER:** Did you ever see what a forty-four magnum pistol can do to a woman's face? —*Taxi Driver*

... burn like arson ...

> **PANCHO:** Knife is good. Is more easy to fix. I got knifed three times. When you're young, everybody sticks knife in you. —*Ride the Pink Horse*

... and sear like a fresh-brewed pot of 7-Eleven coffee splashed in your face ...

> **PERRY SMITH:** I thought Mr. Clutter was a very nice gentleman. ... I thought so right up until the time I cut his throat. —*In Cold Blood*

The words of film noir aren't packing peanuts like the words between crashes in *The Fast and the Furious*, or the bubble wrap of English before and after the explosions in *Armageddon*. They *are* the crashes. They *are* the explosions. They are howls of lust and electric shocks of greed, with quotations and dialog so overheated you could cook a frozen Tombstone pizza on them.

The language of film noir is the only cinematic language that caresses evil with the slow loving care of shoe fetishist locked inside a Manolo Blahnik warehouse, like Noah Cross in *Chinatown*, when he gloats to PI Jake Gittes: "See, Mr. Gitts [sic], most people never have to face the fact that, at the right time and the right place, they're capable of anything."

If French is the language of love, film noir is the language of losers. The language in these operas of desperation is the chipped sequins on Elvis's jumpsuit, the bourbon on the cornflakes, the tarantula in the shorts. No one takes a victory lap here.

Noir poster boy Jeff Bailey in *Out of the Past* knows what it's like to live in that kind of world that's swallowing him like a python. "Is there a way to win?" Kathie Moffat asks him. "There's a way to lose more slowly," he says. If life were a food pyramid, Kathie and Jeff would be the saturated fats.

Right next to them in loser's lane would be Al Roberts in *Detour*. "That's life," über-schmuck Roberts says. "Whichever way you turn, fate sticks out a foot to trip you." When it comes to losers, film noir has more of them than Powerball.

No other species of movie spells out the buffet complex—the desire for everything—with the drooling covetousness Daphne does in *Sleep, My Love*: "We've got a lot—but we haven't got everything. I want what she's got. All of it. I want her house, her name, her man. And I want them now. Tonight."

You Talkin' to Me?

The language of noir is also a telephone tap into the dark side of popular culture in America. Decade by decade it records the panic and loss of men and women trapped in a world that treats them like mutts who overstayed their welcome at the pound. Film noir is always about the same things, the way religion is always about the same things: Sex. Violence. Money. The thin red thong that separates right from wrong.

These themes never really change, but the way we talk about them does. Noir talk in 2005 is as different from what it was in 1975 or 1965 or 1955 as hot pants are from poodle skirts. In the bickering and pillow talk of film noir, every decade leaves clues to what made it tick — the same way a murder can leave a telltale spatter of blood.

The older noirs, the ur-noirs, the first ones in dalmatian black and white, had to be stealth bombers of things unseen and unsaid on the screen. The 1930 Hollywood Production Code (aka the Hays Code) forbade the use of words and phrases like *alley cat*, *bat*, *slut*, *whore*, and *broad* when used for women. You couldn't utter "sex appeal" or tell traveling-salesman jokes, or induce the "sympathy of the audience" to "the side of crime, wrongdoing, evil or sin." Elia Kazan flipped the code the bird with his 1951 version of *A Streetcar Named Desire*, and Otto Preminger monstered it two years later using the words *virgin*, *mistress*, and *pregnant* in *The Moon Is Blue*. But it was the noir classics like *Double Indemnity*, *Gilda*, and *Out of the Past* that really went ninja on the code.

In the Mood for Murder

In the 1944 America of *Double Indemnity*, the right of women to vote was younger than *Ms.* magazine is now. Four hundred thousand women went to war, and seven million went to work. (The Equal Pay Act wasn't passed by Congress until 1963.) Brenda Starr and Wonder Woman debuted — and in 1949 they were singing "Diamonds Are a Girl's Best Friend." Yet it was also a place where a wartime propaganda poster could show a wedding-night-innocent gamine next to a Moses-like injunction: "This is America, where the family is a sacred institution and where children love, honor, and respect their parents. Where a man's home is his castle." Where women sprayed themselves with Avon's Here's My Heart and sniffled into pink Kleenex at *National Velvet*. Meanwhile, film noir language reflected a pre-Kinsey American woman who was like the brothel the town elders visit but won't admit exists. Her patter could heat up faster than a Zippo. "Such a hard name to remember. And such an easy one to forget," Tijuana bible–bodied Gilda taunts square-jawed Johnny Farrell about his white-socks moniker in the eponymous movie. *Scarlet Street*'s Kitty March had more bitch in her than the American Kennel Club: "How can a man be so dumb … I've been waiting to laugh in your face ever since first I met you. You're old and ugly and I'm sick of you. Sick, sick, sick." And *Out of the Past*'s Kathie Moffat tosses men like Pete Rose throws dice. "She can't be all bad," one näif says of the skankosaurus Moffat, "No one is." Jeff Bailey—the pastry Moffat eats for breakfast—knows better. "Well, she comes the closest," he says.

In that pre-cable America, the words *sociopath* and *genocide* were as fresh as new milk. They were the kinds of words that fit Phyllis Dietrichson in *Double Indemnity* like a pair of mink handcuffs. She set the gold standard as the Eve of web-spinning, lie-telling, husband-liquidating, death-loving sluts:

> **PHYLLIS DIETRICHSON:** You see what I mean, Walter?
>
> **WALTER NEFF:** Sure. I've got good eyesight. You mean you want him to have the policy without him knowing it. And that means without the insurance company knowing that he doesn't know it. That's the setup, isn't it?
>
> **PHYLLIS DIETRICHSON:** Is there anything wrong with it?

Is there anything wrong with it? Phyllis's evilocity breaks the sound barrier with at least two husbands dead and Walter shot. She was the clone of Annie Laurie Starr in *Deadly Is the Female*, a draggle-tail and a firearms fanatic who sucks poor, dumb Bart Tare down into her designer slimepit. Tare's too busy slobbering over her like a Saint Bernard to notice the whole relationship smells like bad cheese. She does away with him with the same offhanded ease with which people brush dandruff off their shoulder. "Come on, Bart," she says, "let's finish it the way we started it: on the level." A level six feet under, she means.

The 1950s: Bombshells Away

If money and sex were the lingua franca of *Double Indemnity* and the 1940s noirs, the bomb and shrunken women were the language of the 1950s. They jutted out of the movies like Jayne Mansfield's bosom. Atom spies Julius and Ethel Rosenberg and Klaus Fuchs infested the country like weevils in bread.

The Soviets exploded a hydrogen bomb in 1953. Senator Joe McCarthy paused between his suppers of Scotch and quarter-pound sticks of butter to authoritatively state there were 205 or 57 or maybe 4 communists in the government.

We combated these godless evils the best way we knew how, by stuffing the country's men into gray flannel suits, adding the phrase *under God* to the Pledge of Allegiance, and packing words into our daily lingo as big as the fins on the cars we drove-words like *thermonuclear*, *strontium 90*, *fallout*, and *doomsday*. The language of noir itself was as fortifying as the food was then, but instead of juicing it with the "morale vitamin," B-12, it was gassed up with the bomb.

Robert Aldrich's *Kiss Me Deadly* understood that. It knew the bomb was just the pagan gods, come down to us in the form of a mushroom cloud. That's why, in *Kiss*, black-market radioactive material is chased like the Golden Fleece and feared like Pandora's box:

> **DR. G.E. SOBERIN:** The head of the Medusa. That's what's in the box. And whoever looks on her will be changed, not into stone, but into brimstone and ashes. Well, of course, you wouldn't believe me. You'd have to see for yourself, wouldn't you?
>
> ⋯⋯⋯⋯⋯⋯⋯⋯⋯⋯⋯⋯⋯⋯⋯⋯⋯⋯⋯⋯⋯⋯⋯⋯⋯⋯⋯⋯⋯⋯⋯⋯
>
> **LILY CARVER:** Whatever is in that box—it must be very precious. So many people have died for it.
>
> **DR. G.E. SOBERIN:** Yes, it is very precious.
>
> **LILY CARVER:** I want half.
>
> **DR. G.E. SOBERIN:** I agree with you. You should have at least half. You deserve it, for all the creature comforts you've given me. But unfortunately, the object in this box cannot be divided.
>
> **LILY CARVER (POINTS GUN):** Then I'll take it all—if you don't mind.
>
> ⋯⋯⋯⋯⋯⋯⋯⋯⋯⋯⋯⋯⋯⋯⋯⋯⋯⋯⋯⋯⋯⋯⋯⋯⋯⋯⋯⋯⋯⋯⋯⋯
>
> **DR. G.E. SOBERIN:** Listen to me as if I were Cerberus barking with all his heads at the gates of Hell. I will tell you where to take it. But don't, don't open the box.

Lily was one of the walking bet-you-can't-eat-just-one, praying mantis exceptions to the 1950s rule: In a movieverse where the ultimate terror was a fifty-foot woman, the ultimate ideal was a woman smaller than *The Incredible Shrinking Man*.

In the '50s, even with the American Medical Association declaring that female hysteria was not really an ailment, the Daughters of Bilitis forming the first lesbian organization in the United States, NASA organizing a female astronaut team, and the Drug Administration approving the first birth control pills, women woke up in an Eisenhower Weirdsville. They dressed in pinched-waist skirts and Cristóbal Balenciaga dresses with soft, round Kim Novak shoulders. Under them they wore Très Sècrete (an "inflatable brassiere with a little plastic straw for blowing it up to the desired size"), slept in babydoll pajamas, and munched on Reserpine, Miltown, and Equanil (the first commercially successful tranquilizers) to plunge back to that fitful sleep.

The homicidal harlots of the 1940s noirs jiggled back to the kitchen, where the men stepped on them like the linoleum floors they stayed home to wax. Between 1945 and 1950, the number of women behind bars went down by 33 percent. There was an equal plummet in the number of females executed in the 1950s from the previous decade. Instead of a shark-souled Phyllis Dietrichson or the Kevlar-hearted Brigid O'Shaughnessy in *The Maltese Falcon*, you had passive-petunia Crystal in *The Blue Gardenia*: "Now me, I've got my life with Homer. Drive-in dinner. Drive-in movie. And afterwards we go for a drive." You've got Icey Spoon in *The Night of the Hunter*: "When you've been married to a man forty years you know [sex] don't amount to a hill of beans. I've been married to my Walt that long and I swear in all that time I just lie there thinking about my canning." And you've also got a walking sperm bank, Rita, in *The Big Combo*: "A woman doesn't care how a guy makes a living, just how he makes love." Bold talk from someone who was now earning less than 56 cents for every dollar a man made.

When noir women weren't speaking "virtuous housewife" in the 1950s, they were talking "victimized floozy." "A scar isn't so bad," says Debby Marsh in *The Big Heat* after boyfriend Vince Stone splashes her face with a pot of hot coffee. "Not if it's only on one side. I can always go through life sideways." Rita, in *Sweet Smell of Success*, asks, "What am I, a bowl of fruit? A tangerine that peels in a minute?"

Film noir X-rayed the skull beneath the skin of Levittown, Barbie dolls, and *Sing Along With Mitch*. This exchange from *Touch of Evil*, which shows the world of good guys/bad guys through shit-colored glasses, must have gone over like a polio outbreak at a public swimming pool:

> **SGT. PETE MENZIES:** You're a killer.
>
> **CAPT. HANK QUINLAN:** Partly. I'm a cop.

Even after local cops busted up the 1957 powwow of organized crime's "commission" in up-state New York, J. Edgar Hoover could barely bring himself to whisper what film noir was shouting: Crime wasn't a Dillinger here or a Capone there; it was a corporation with more gray flannel suits than guns. Alec Stiles brags in *The Street With No Name* that he's building his Crime-Mart organization along "scientific principles." An offended mug in *Force of Evil* says, "What do you mean 'gangsters'? It's business." The upstart crook Colleoni in *Brighton Rock* sniffs "I'm a businessman." In *The Long Wait*, a thug reminds his co-thug, who wants to knock off the guy he thinks is sexing up his girl, "This isn't personal, this is business," and an enforcer explains to an outnumbered cop in the tones companies reserve for disgruntled shareholders, "You're just one guy buckin' a big company. It don't matter if you beat my brains out or not. We're in business for keeps."

The 1960s: Noir a–Go(ne)–Go(ne)

Film noir dropped into a coma in the 1960s, like a PI with one too many concussions. Look at the American Film Institute's roll call of the one hundred greatest films: Of the twelve that appeared between 1941–1950, at least four (33 percent) were noirs. Of the eighteen that came out between 1961–1970, just one (5.5 percent) was a noir. The Internet Movie Database (www.IMDb.com) counts 151 movies in the 1950s as noir. (They consider *Touch of Evil* in 1958 the last noir. Maybe they thought noir bought a shovel and buried itself, like saddle shoes and panty raids.) But IMDb classifies twenty-three movies in the 1960s as neo-noirs. Film noir had slowed to the pace of gun control legislation in a Republican administration.

Maybe it was because the movies in the 1960s used wide-screen filming techniques like Cinerama and CinemaScope to compete with television. Their depressingly cheery tie-dyed colors elbowed out the casket blacks and candlelight whites of traditional noir. Maybe noir was knocked unconscious by a cultural mugger whose insipid vocabulary clashed with noir as badly as Birkenstocks and granny glasses would with a trench coats and fedoras: *love beads*, *sock it to me*, *diet cola*, *Nehru jackets*, *groovy*, and *folk rock*.

Maybe the real culprit was the Hollywood Production Code. The lack of it, anyway. When the code went RIP in 1966, film noir—previously a ghetto for taboo subjects—party-crashed mainstream movies like *Bonnie and Clyde*, *The Wild Bunch*, and *The Dirty Dozen* with a kind of "Is that a death squad in your pocket or are you just happy to see me?" leer, while *Midnight Cowboy* opened up a can of David Lynch: "You want the word on that brother- and sister-act? Hansel's a fag and Gretel's got the hots for herself, so who cares, right? Load up on the salami." Like striptease and country music years later, we tossed film noir into the Great American Blander and served it up as a Happy Meal for the mainstream.

Only *The Naked Kiss*, *Cape Fear*, *Point Blank*, and *The Manchurian Candidate*, which smokes with a humor so dark you need a flashlight to watch it, kept the nightmare alive. An Alice's looking glass of popular misconceptions and urban legends, *The Manchurian Candidate* playfully warped reports that Chinese captors had reprogrammed American POWs during the Korean War in less time than it takes to reboot your PC. "His brain has not only been washed, as they say," a Dr. Frankensteinski gloats over the human killbot he's created, "it has been dry-cleaned."

The rest of the noirs in the '60s were just an aging AAA farm team trying out for the majors. Like *The Money Trap*, which briefly reunited Glenn Ford and Rita Hayworth, post-*Gilda*: In its mini-skirt shortness, it staggered about like the director shot it with a tranquilizer dart. Just six years after *The Manchurian Candidate*, in which Frank Sinatra moves with the intensity of a man who just found out his life insurance company cancelled his policy the same day his doctor diagnosed him with terminal cancer, Sinatra walked through 1968's *Lady in Cement* with the speed of a man wearing concrete Florsheims. Like plastic flowers on a marble tombstone, the '60s noirs looked cheap and tawdry.

Except for the Ronald Reagan version of *The Killers*—perversely watchable because the Gipper pimp-slaps Camelot-camp-follower Angie Dickenson around—they were about as thrilling as finding a pair of khaki pants in the Gap.

Like Sigmund Freud, film noir didn't know what women wanted anymore. How could it, when even the reliable Maidenform "I Dreamed" bra ad campaign (including 1959's "I dreamed I sang a duet at the Met in my Maidenform bra") was finally unhooked in 1969 after a twenty-year run?

Noir tried a reformed bald hooker in *The Naked Kiss* and the Teutonic Barbie doll Elke Sommer in *The Money Trap*, but it just wasn't the same. Neither one wore the Eau de Hellfire that Phyllis Dietrichson in *Double Indemnity*, Cora Smith in *The Postman Always Rings Twice*, Myrna in *On Dangerous Ground*, Dodie in *Appointment With Danger*, and Kathie Moffat in *Out of the Past* bought by the gallon at Costco. Women in '60s noirs couldn't be the soft bullets of the 1940s. They couldn't be the overstuffed Jessica Rabbits of the 1950s. They just couldn't be.

The 1970s: It's a Noir World, After All

On June 13, 1971, America officially went back on Central Cynical Time. That was the day the *New York Times* published the Pentagon Papers, the secret government study of how we duped and deluded our way into the Vietnam War. That revelation was followed by a Tet offensive of slang that muscled its way into the country's lexicon: *Watergate, Plumbers, smoking gun, expletive deleted, mistakes were made,* and *follow the money.* When you add the glowing example of Three Mile Island, it was plain that the institutions film noir had always sniped at like sharpshooters were worse than anyone imagined.

The country understood that the social contract—not just a few rogue cops in *Touch of Evil* or *The Mob*—had been abandoned like South Vietnam: the percentage of Americans who said they "trust the Government to do what is right" dropped from 75 percent in 1958 to 36 percent in 1974.

So we jumped back on film noir like it was the last chopper out of a burning Saigon. And somewhere Honoré de Balzac was laughing like a mental patient. "Behind every great fortune, there is a crime," the nineteenth-century author of *La Comédie Humaine* wrote. Fortune and crime were coming out of the pores of 1974's *Chinatown* like the water its vulpine Noah Cross stole. His eyes gleaming like Satan's highbeams and voice croaking with rigor mortis, Cross's speech is a witch's brew of Rotary Club and Rasputin:

> **JAKE GITTES:** No, I just want to know what you're worth. Over $10 million?
>
> **NOAH CROSS:** Oh my, yes.
>
> **JAKE GITTES:** Why are you doing it? How much better can you eat? What can you buy that you can't already afford?
>
> **NOAH CROSS:** The future, Mr. Gitts [sic], the future.

The noir of the 1940s and 1950s had shed its aging skin. *Chinatown*'s cinematography used sunlight like *The Big Combo* and *Detour* used shadow: as a way to cloak its malefactors and devour its victims. Noir's tropes—the PI as patsy, the rich as reptiles, the *femme* as *fatale*—were reborn in its language. The tommy-gun speech of *White Heat* and *Force of Evil* ran out of ammunition; film noir reloaded with the I'd-like-to-buy-the-world-a-Coke, smile button-y patter of Philip Marlowe's incessant "It's okay with me" in the 1973 remake of *The Long Goodbye* and the I'm-late-for-my-nap cadence of a Mylanta-challenged Marlowe in the 1978 copy of *The Big Sleep* (which the producers must have made at Kinko's).

Then screenwriter Paul Schrader's script for *Taxi Driver* tore the skin off bland-leading-the-bland movies like, *Rocky* and anything with Jill Clayburgh, and wore it like a Jim Henson Muppet suit. *Taxi Driver*'s all-American psychopath, Travis Bickle, spewed his way into the cultural ROM with his "You talkin' to me?" soliloquy. (It ranks as the ninth most famous line in movie history.)

By the time Bickle's meth'ed acting wound down, Schrader had stripped the taboos off language in movies like the skin of a duck hanging upside down in a Chinatown butcher shop. Bickle's homicidal rant is the era's bumper sticker, summing up a murder rate that had doubled from the mid-1960s to the late 1970s, and that had peaked in 1980 at 10.2 per 100,000 in population.

And after his middle-finger tirade against the world, the word *fuck* became the duct tape of movie talk:

TRAVIS BICKLE: Faster than you, you fuckin' son of a … I saw you comin', you fuck, shit-heel. I'm standin' here. You make the move. You make the move. It's your move. Don't try it, you fucker. You talkin' to me? You talkin' to me? You talkin' to me? Well, who the hell else are you talkin' to? You talkin' to me? Well, I'm the only one here. Who the fuck do you think you're talkin' to? Oh, yeah? Huh? OK. Huh? Listen you fuckers, you screwheads. Here is a man who would not take it anymore. Who would not let … listen you fuckers, you screwheads. Here is a man who would not take it anymore. A man who stood up against the scum, the cunts, the dogs, the filth, the shit, here is someone who stood up. Here is: you're dead.

The 1980s—2000s: It's the Mammon, Stupid

Taxi Driver and *Chinatown* gave movies a cinematic Heimlich. We needed the practice for the era of choking on "Greed is good," *The Official Preppy Handbook*, "yuppification," 14 percent mortgage rates in 1981 (followed by a 14 percent poverty rate in 1982), "the one who dies with the most toys wins," the House of Representatives writing more than 8,000 bad checks on their own congressional bank, $182 billion to bail out the nation's savings and loan industry, and the top executives from the 25 largest corporate bankruptcies of the last decade limo-ing away $3.3 billion from the sale of their stock and other payments while their businesses dropkicked more than 88,000 people out of their jobs.

After all this, film noir watched America like a gambler eyeing the dealer in a crooked card game. Film noir converted to the Church of Follow the Money. *Miller's Crossing*, *A Simple Plan*, *The Spanish Prisoner*, *Thief*, *Blood Simple*, *52 Pick-Up*, *House of Games*, *The Underneath*, *Fargo*, *Heat*, and *Heist* scratched chalk outlines around the financial crimes and criminals of the time. Noir stalked the cash and discovered everyone had it but you and me. "Self-styled masters of the universe," spews Monty Brogan in *25th Hour*. "Michael Douglas Gordon Gekko wannabe motherfuckers, figuring out new ways to rob hardworking people blind. Send those Enron assholes to jail for fucking life."

You didn't need the American Bankruptcy Institute to know bankruptcy filings had risen 500 percent since 1980, or that money laundering had scuttled higher and faster than Enron's stock price. Now all you needed was to hear Sarah Mitchell in *A Simple Plan*. "What about me?" she gripes to her husband. "Spending the rest of my life, eight hours a day, with a fake smile plastered on my face, checking out books and then coming home to cook dinner for you, the same meals over and over again, whatever the week's coupons will allow, only going out to restaurants for special occasions—birthdays or anniversaries—and even then having to watch what we order, skipping the appetizer, coming home for dessert. You think that's going to make me happy?" What would keep her happy wasn't keeping up with the Joneses; it was keeping up with the Gateses.

If the American dream of financial security had morphed into a nightmare of endless soirées at Red Lobster, any remaining taboos about sex and women disappeared into irrelevance like eight-track tape players. Women needed men like nursing homes needed pneumonia: The number of single mothers increased by more than 300 percent between 1970 and 2000. In *The Blue Gardenia* in 1953, Crystal's philosophy— "Honey, if a girl killed every man who got fresh with her, how much of the male population do you think there'd be left?"—helps explain why fewer than 2 percent of all prisoners then were women; today the number has more than quadrupled to almost 7 percent. (Today, Crystal would be one of the *Golden Girls*, but with more stripes in her wardrobe.) And if women could get *G.I. Jane*-y with the U.S. military (fully integrating with the men in 1973) and crash the XY-only Supreme Court party (the first female justice joined in 1981), then why not get all equal rights on the frat house known as death row? In 1990, 35 women were on the DR; by 2000, that number had gone up by 55 percent to 54.

All this time, the women in *Deadly Is the Female*, *Detour*, *Double Indemnity*, and *Out of the Past* had a higher purpose as a swarm of snake-haired Henry Higginses for the likes of Matty Walker in *Body Heat* ("You aren't too bright. I like that in a man.") and the sexual Terminatrix Bridget Gregory in *The Last Seduction* ("I'm trying to decide whether you're a total bitch or not," says one chump-of-the-month. "I'm a total fucking bitch," she explains.). These *femmes horribles* of the 1980s and 1990s had more balls than Spalding and more ambition than Stalin at Yalta. Like their black-and-white ancestors, they reeled in men whose only job in life was contributing to the Encyclopedia of Fuck-Ups: "Lazy? Ugly? Horny?" Ned Racine says in *Body Heat*. "I got 'em all." What happened to men? It wasn't just that they were eating 20.5 pounds less red

14

meat a year and switching to omega-3 fatty acids and alfalfa sprouts, and then brushing after every meal with Colgate herbal toothpaste. It wasn't that they made up 29 percent of all spa goers. It wasn't even that men had to be men anymore: "Thing is, though, you're not a girl," Fergus explains to Dil in *The Crying Game*. "Details, baby, details," says Dil. Maybe what happened was the makeup. When it became crueler, it meant the women had become meaner. Urban Decay started selling cosmetics with names like Roach, Smog, Rust, Oil Slick, and Acid Rain under the tagline "Does Pink Make You Puke?" to women who, in the 1950s, would have used Betty Crocker mixes to bake their "heart-warming muffins of long ago."

But the noir women in the 1990s and 2000s had sperm-and-egged it with the male emotional iceboxes of the '50s to produce a new model that was impossibly all curves and yet all edges:

SUE THE BARTENDER: Well, well. It's been a long time, Cork.

CORKY: Five years, two months, sixteen days. How ya doing, Sue?

SUE THE BARTENDER: Like shit. Well, now that we're all caught up, can I buy you a drink?

....

CORKY: To me, stealing's always been a lot like sex. Two people who want the same thing: They get in a room, they talk about it. They start to plan. It's kind of like flirting. It's kind of like foreplay, 'cause the more they talk about it, the wetter they get. —***Bound***

....

BRIDGET GREGORY: You're my designated fuck.

MIKE SWALE: Designated fuck? They make cards for that? What if I want to be more than your designated fuck?

BRIDGET GREGORY: I'll designate someone else. —***The Last Seduction***

....

EDWARD "ED" CRANE: It was only a couple of weeks later she suggested we get married. I said, "Don't you want to get to know me more?" She said, "Why? Does it get better?" —***The Man Who Wasn't There***

It does get better. The language of film noir will always have more pricks than acupuncture, more punches than the Golden Gloves, more venom than marriage counseling.

If, as Emerson said, "Language is fossil poetry," film noir will now and forever be a skeletal record of monsters that bite worse than any T. rex.

This is L.A. This is my town. Out here you're a trespasser. Out here I can pick you up, burn your house, —MAX HOOVER fuck your wife, and kill your dog.

Mulholland Falls
1996

CHAPTER

ONE

The Dicks and the Desperate

1941–1950

They Drive by Night [1940]

LANA CARLSEN: Your liver must look like a bomb hit it.

ED J. CARLSEN: Well, you know what I say: live and let liver.

I Wake Up Screaming [1941]

FRANKIE CHRISTOPHER: I wouldn't touch you with sterilized gloves.

POLICE INSP. ED CORNELL: When I get all my evidence together, I'm gonna have you tied up, like a pig in a slaughterhouse.

....

POLICE INSP. ED CORNELL: I nick a guy on my own time, send him up to the chair, then I get back pay.

FRANKIE CHRISTOPHER: Must be a great life. Like a garbage man, only with people.

....

POLICE INSP. ED CORNELL: I'll get you eventually. If not tomorrow, next week. If not next week, next year. Time's nothing in my life. It is in yours. Each minute's an eternity to a man in your shoes.

....

POLICE INSP. ED CORNELL: I'll follow you into your grave. I'll write my name on your tombstone.

The Maltese Falcon [1941]

SAM SPADE: My guess might be excellent or it might be crummy, but Mrs. Spade didn't raise any children dippy enough to make guesses in front of a district attorney, and an assistant district attorney, and a stenographer.

....

JOEL CAIRO: You always have a very smooth explanation ready.

SAM SPADE: What do you want me to do, learn to stutter?

....

SAM SPADE: I don't mind a reasonable amount of trouble.

The Shanghai Gesture [1941]

DR. OMAR: I cheat at everything, except cards.

....

DR. OMAR: I can say with pride I've never paid for anything in my life.

....

DR. OMAR: In short, I'm a thoroughbred mongrel.

I want you to know
I couldn't be fonder of you if you were my own son.
But, well,
if you lose a son,
it's possible to get another.
There's only one Maltese Falcon.

—KASPER GUTMAN

The Maltese Falcon 1941

The Glass Key [1942]

RUSTY: My first wife was a second cook in a third-rate joint on Fourth Street.

Shadow of a Doubt [1943]

UNCLE CHARLIE: You think you know something, don't you? You think you're the clever little girl who knows something. There's so much you don't know ... so much. What do you know really? You're just an ordinary little girl living in an ordinary little town.

You wake up every morning of your life and you know perfectly well that there's nothing in the world to trouble you. You go through your ordinary little day and at night you sleep your untroubled, ordinary little sleep filled with peaceful, stupid dreams ... and I brought you nightmares.

Laura [1944]

WALDO LYDECKER: How singularly innocent I look this morning.

WALDO LYDECKER: I'm not kind, I'm vicious. It's the secret of my charm.

WALDO LYDECKER: I am the most widely misquoted man in America.

WALDO LYDECKER: I don't use a pen. I write with a goose quill dipped in venom.

BESSIE CLARY: I ain't afraid of cops. I was brought up to spit whenever I saw one.

DET. LT. MARK MCPHERSON: OK, go ahead and spit if that'll make you feel better.

SHELBY CARPENTER: I can afford a blemish on my character, but not on my clothes.

The Lost Weekend [1945]

DON BIRNAM: Don Birnam is dead already. He died over this weekend.

HELEN ST. JAMES: Did he? What did he die of?

DON BIRNAM: Of a lot of things. Of alcohol. Of moral anemia. Fear. Shame. DTs.

....

DON BIRNAM [TO BARTENDER]: It shrinks my liver, doesn't it? It pickles my kidneys, yeah. But what does it do to my mind? It tosses the sandbags overboard so the balloon can soar. Suddenly I'm above the ordinary. I'm competent, supremely competent. I'm walking a tightrope over Niagara Falls. I'm one of the great ones. I'm Michelangelo, molding the beard of Moses. I'm Van Gogh painting pure sunlight. I'm Horowitz, playing the Emperor Concerto. I'm John Barrymore before the movies got him by the throat. I'm Jesse James and his two brothers, all three of them. I'm W. Shakespeare. And out there it's not Third Avenue any longer, it's the Nile. Nat. The Nile and down it moves the barge of Cleopatra.

Mildred Pierce [1945]

VEDA PIERCE: I love you mother, really I do. But let's not be sticky about it.

Scarlet Street [1945]

KITTY MARCH: Who do you think you are? My guardian angel?

MILLIE RAY: Not me, honey. I lost those wings a long time ago.

The Big Sleep [1946]

GEN. STERNWOOD: You may smoke, too. I can still enjoy the smell of it. Nice state of affairs when a man has to indulge his vices by proxy. You're looking, sir, at a very dull survival of a very gaudy life.

....

GEN. STERNWOOD: I seem to exist largely on heat, like a newborn spider.

....

GEN. STERNWOOD: Do you like orchids?

PHILIP MARLOWE: Not particularly.

GEN. STERNWOOD: Nasty things. Their flesh is too much like the flesh of men, and their perfume has the rotten sweetness of corruption.

I reserve my

vices

for after business hours.

—VICTOR JAMES COLEBROOKE

Wanted for
Murder 1946

PHILIP MARLOWE: I don't mind if you don't like my manners, I don't like them myself. They're pretty bad. I grieve over them long winter evenings. And I don't mind your ritzing me or drinking your lunch out of a bottle. But don't waste your time trying to cross-examine me.

GEN. STERNWOOD: If I seem a bit sinister as a parent, Mr. Marlowe, it's because my hold on life is too slight to include any Victorian hypocrisy. I need hardly add that any man who has lived as I have and who indulges for the first time in parenthood at my age deserves all he gets.

GENERAL STERNWOOD: How do you like your brandy, sir?

PHILIP MARLOWE: In a glass.

VIVIAN STERNWOOD RUTLEDGE: Why did you have to go on?

PHILIP MARLOWE: Too many people told me to stop.

Black Angel [1946]

MARKO: I don't slug and you don't think. Is that a deal?

The Blue Dahlia [1946]

BUZZ WANCHEK: Bourbon straight, with a bourbon chaser.

LEO: Just don't get too complicated, Eddie. When a man gets too complicated, he's unhappy. And when he's unhappy, his luck runs out.

The Dark Corner [1946]

HARDY CATHCART: How I detest the dawn. The grass always looks like it's been left out all night.

BRADFORD GALT: No, I'm clean as a peeled egg.

BRADFORD GALT: I can be framed easier than Whistler's Mother.

BRADFORD GALT: There goes my last lead. I feel all dead inside. I'm backed up in a dark corner, and I don't know who's hitting me.

The Killers [1946]

NICK ADAMS: Why do they want to kill you?

OLE "THE SWEDE" ANDERSEN/PETE LUND: I did something wrong . . . once.

The Postman Always Rings Twice [1946]

FRANK CHAMBERS: Well, so long mister. Thanks for the ride, the three cigarettes and for not laughing at my theories on life.

The Strange Love of Martha Ivers [1946]

SAILOR: Where are we?

SAM MASTERSON: In a small accident.

SAILOR: What happened?

SAM MASTERSON: The road curved but I didn't.

WALTER P. O'NEIL: Couldn't you see blackmail in his eyes?

MARTHA IVERS: I haven't your experience with criminals.

Born to Kill [1947]

MARTY WATERMAN: If we're going to carry on a conversation, it'd help for you to talk.

Brute Force [1947]

DR. WALTERS: Force does make leaders. But you forget one thing: it also destroys them.

Crossfire [1947]

CAPT. FINLAY: Hating is always the same, always senseless. One day it kills Irish Catholics, the next day Jews. The next day Protestants. The next day Quakers. It's hard to stop. It can end up killing men who wear striped neckties. Or people from Tennessee.

....

CAPT. FINLAY: You still don't know where he is?

SGT. PETER KEELEY: No. I didn't know when I came in here, and I haven't suddenly gotten any brighter.

....

MONTGOMERY: 'Course, ... met a lot of guys like him.

CAPT. FINLAY: Like what?

MONTGOMERY: Oh, you know. Guys that played it safe during the war, prance around keepin' themselves in civvies, swell apartments, swell dames ... you know the kind.

CAPT. FINLAY: I'm not sure that I do. Just what kind?

MONTGOMERY: Well, you know, some of 'em are named Samuels, some of 'em got funnier names.

....

SGT. PETER KEELEY: He oughta look at a casualty list sometime. There's a lot of funny names there, too.

Kiss of Death [1947]

TOMMY UDO: Imagine me in on this cheap rap, big man like me. Picked up just for shovin' a guy's ears off his head. Traffic ticket stuff.

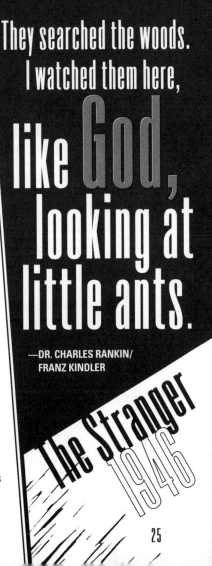

They searched the woods. I watched them here, like GOD, looking at little ants.

—DR. CHARLES RANKIN/ FRANZ KINDLER

The Stranger 1946

The Lady From Shanghai [1947]

ARTHUR BANNISTER: George, that's the first time anyone ever thought enough of you to call you a shark. You were a good lawyer you'd be flattered.

Lady in the Lake [1947]

ADRIENNE FROMSETT: I don't like your manner.

PHILIP MARLOWE: I'm not selling it.

ADRIENNE FROMSETT: I need help.

PHILIP MARLOWE: Like I need four thumbs.

Nightmare Alley [1947]

ZEENA KRUMBEIN: Look at him. Like a dog waiting for somebody to throw him a bone.

McGRAW: You know what a geek is don't you?

STANTON CARLISLE: Yeah. Sure I … I know what a geek is.

McGRAW: You think you can handle it?

STANTON CARLISLE: Mister, I was made for it.

CARNY WORKER: How can a guy get so low?

McGRAW: He reached too high.

LILITH RITTER: I think you're a perfectly normal human being. Selfish and ruthless when you want something. Generous and kindly when you've got it.

Out of the Past [1947]

WHIT STERLING: My feelings? About ten years ago, I hid them somewhere and haven't been able to find them.

WHIT STERLING: Besides, Joe couldn't find a prayer in the Bible.

Quai des Orfèvres [1947] aka *Jenny Lamour*

INSP. ANTOINE: We move in all kinds of circles, meet all sorts of people. I learned engraving from a counterfeiter, accounting from a swindler. A taxi dancer tried to teach me the tango. But nothing doing. It wasn't up my alley.

Singapore [1947]

MR. MAURIBUS: I like troubled times. They keep the police occupied.

T-Men [1947]

NARRATOR: They had to know all the answers. Failure to do so would mean a bad grade later on in the shape of a bullet or an ice pick.

THE SCHEMER: You think you'll get a fair shake from this crowd? When cows give beer you will.

Force of Evil [1948]

JOE MORSE: You tell me the story of your life and maybe I can suggest a happy ending.

He Walked by Night [1948]

NARRATOR: No one in the underworld recognized that mysterious face. He was as unknown as if he had lived in the sixteenth century.

NARRATOR: The work of the police, like that of woman, is never done.

Key Largo [1948]

FRANK McCLOUD: Johnny Rocco was more than a king. He was an emperor. His rule extended over beer, slot machines, the numbers racket, and a dozen other for-

I didn't have enough strength to resist **corruption,** but I was strong enough to **fight** for a piece of it.

—JOE MORSE

Force of Evil 1948

bidden enterprises. He was a master of the fix. Whom he couldn't corrupt, he terrified. Whom he couldn't terrify, he murdered.

- -

JOHNNY ROCCO: Well, listen, soldier. Thousands of guys got guns but there's only one Johnny Rocco.

- -

FRANK McCLOUD: You don't like it, do you, Rocco, the storm? Show it your gun, why don't you? If it doesn't stop, shoot it.

Pitfall [1948]

MONA STEVENS: You're a little man with a briefcase. You go to work every morning and you do as you're told.

The Street With No Name [1948]

ROBERT DANKER: I told you I was in Chicago that night.

INSP. GEORGE A. BRIGGS: Have you any proof of that?

ROBERT DANKER: Sure, I cut off my arm and buried it there for an alibi. All you got to do is go dig it up.

Abandoned [1949]

MARK SITKO: You going legitimate is like a vulture turning vegetarian.

- -

KERRIC: I was just thinking how nice life used to be when I stuck to blackmail and petty larceny.

Beyond the Forest [1949]

ROSA MOLINE: What a dump.

The Bribe [1949]

RIGBY: I never knew a crooked road could look so straight.

Criss Cross [1949]

DET. LT. PETE RAMIREZ: I shoulda been a better friend. I shoulda stopped you. I shoulda grabbed you by the neck. I shoulda kicked your teeth in.

Impact [1949]

WALTER WILLIAMS: I'll never think of our moments together without nausea.

Rope of Sand [1949]

NARRATOR: This part of the desert of South Africa, where only a parched camel thorn tree relieves the endless parallels of time, space, and sky, surrounds like a rope of sand the richest diamond-bearing area in the world—an uneasy land where men inflamed by monotony and the heat sometimes forget the rules of civilization.

....

TOADY: I was only thinking if, uh, if ever you meet this young man, this guide, you might deliver a message for me.

MIKE DAVIS: Saying what?

TOADY: Oh, saying, um, saying that I am here, free as the wind, fountain of extraordinary knowledge, splendidly corrupt and eager to be of profitable service.

The Third Man [1949]

HOLLY MARTINS: Have you ever seen any of your victims?

HARRY LIME: You know, I never feel comfortable on these sort of things. Victims? Don't be melodramatic. Tell me [LOOKS DOWN ON THE CROWD FROM A FERRIS WHEEL], Would you really feel any pity if one of those dots stopped moving forever? If I offered you twenty thousand pounds for every dot that stopped, would you really, old man, tell me to keep my money? Or would you calculate how many dots you could afford to spare? Free of income tax, old man. Free of income tax—the only way you can save money nowadays.

White Heat [1949]

VERNA JARRETT: Always "somebody tipped them off." Never "the cops are smart."

The Asphalt Jungle [1950]

POLICE COMM. HARDY: People are being cheated, robbed, murdered, raped. And that goes on twenty-four hours a day, every day in the year. And that's not exceptional, that's usual. It's the same in every city in the modern world. But suppose we had no police force, good or bad. Suppose we had ... just silence. Nobody to listen, nobody to answer. The battle's finished. The jungle wins. The predatory beasts take over.

....

DOC RIEDENSCHNEIDER: Experience has taught me never to trust a policeman. Just when you think one's all right, he turns legit.

In a Lonely Place [1950]

SYLVIA NICOLAI: Well, he's exciting because he isn't quite normal.

DET. SGT. BRUB NICOLAI: Maybe us cops could use some of that brand of abnormality. I learned more about this case in five minutes from him than I did from all of our photographs, tire prints and investigations.

....

DIXON STEELE: It was his story against mine, but of course, I told my story better.

Kiss Tomorrow Goodbye [1950]

RALPH COTTER: And now, would one fugitive from justice care to fix another fugitive from justice ... a sandwich?

Night and the City [1950]

KRISTO: You're very sharp, Mr. Fabian. You've done a very sharp thing, maybe even sharp enough to cut your throat.

I don't **pray.**

Kneeling bags my nylons.

—LORRAINE MINOSA

Ace in the Hole 1951

Sunset Boulevard [1950]

JOE GILLIS: You're Norma Desmond. Used to be in silent pictures. Used to be big.

NORMA DESMOND: I am big. It's the pictures that got small.

....

NORMA DESMOND: They took the idols and smashed them, the Fairbankses, the Gilberts, the Valentinos. And who've we got now? Some no-bodies.

....

NORMA DESMOND: We didn't need dialogue. We had faces.

....

JOE GILLIS: I didn't know you were planning a comeback.

NORMA DESMOND: I hate that word. It's a re-turn, a return to the millions of people who have never forgiven me for deserting the screen.

....

JOE GILLIS: Oh, wake up, Norma, you'd be killing yourself to an empty house. The audi-ence left twenty years ago. Now face it.

....

JOE GILLIS: There's nothing tragic about being fifty. Not unless you're trying to be twenty-five.

....

NORMA DESMOND [STARES INTO NEWSREEL CAMERA]: And I promise you I'll never desert you again because after "Salome" we'll make another picture and another picture. You see, this is my life. It always will be.

It's a Bitter Little World

Nothing else. Just us, the cameras, and those wonderful people out there in the dark. All right, Mr. DeMille, I'm ready for my close-up.

The Underworld Story [1950]

CATHERINE HARRIS: Did you ever rob graves, Mr. Reese?

MIKE REESE: No future in it.

Where the Sidewalk Ends [1950]

TOMMY SCALISE: It's always a pleasure to watch a cop's foreplay.

1951–1960

Ace in the Hole [1951]

REPORTER: We're all in the same boat.

CHARLES "CHUCK" TATUM: I'm in the boat. You're in the water. Now let's see how you can swim.

....

LORRAINE MINOSA: I've met a lot of hardboiled eggs in my time, but you— you're twenty minutes.

....

CHARLES "CHUCK" TATUM: I've done a lot of lying in my time. I've lied to men who wear belts. I've lied to men who wear suspenders. But I'd never be so stupid as to lie to a man who wears both belt and suspenders.

....

CHARLES "CHUCK" TATUM: I can handle big news and little news. And if there's no news, I'll go out and bite a dog.

Appointment With Danger [1951]

JOE REGAS: You look like you just lost your best friend.

AL GODDARD: I'm my best friend.

JOE REGAS: That's what I said.

....

MAURY AHEARN: You've been chasing hoodlums for so long, you don't know how to treat ordinary people. Warm up, will ya?

AL GODDARD: Sure, I'll fall in love for you.

MAURY AHEARN: I don't think you could because you don't know what a love affair is.

AL GODDARD: It's what goes on between a man and a forty-five pistol that won't jam.

....

SISTER AUGUSTINE: You know, Mr. Goddard, with a little practice you could be a nice man.

AL GODDARD: I'll take two weeks off sometime and try it.

Cry Danger [1951]

LOUIE CASTRO: You know, big men don't scare easy.

ROCKY MULLOY: Then big men must get popped off pretty regularly.

....

DELONG: Well, place looks lived in.

ROCKY MULLOY: Yeah, but by what?

....

ROCKY MULLOY: Have you read that book, "What to Do Until the Police Come"?

The Mob [1951]

POLICE COMMISSIONER: A man commits a murder right in front of your own eyes. You tip your hat, shine his shoes, and send him off with his hot little gun still in his hands.

....

POLICE COMMISSIONER: Instead of actually suspending you, we're going to give you a chance to get yourself killed.

If you want to
play with
matches,
that's your business.
But not in gas-filled rooms.
—FRANK JESSUP

Angel Face 1952

Prisons are bulging with dummies who wonder how they got there.
—MIKE LAGANA

The Big Heat 1953

DET. JOHNNY DAMICO: I have to go underground. You know, like gophers and communists.

The Prowler [1951]

SUSAN GILVRAY: You don't like bein' a policeman, do you?

WEBB GARWOOD: Why should I?

SUSAN GILVRAY: Well, for one thing, you look nice in a uniform.

Strangers on a Train [1951]

GUY HAINES: Doesn't that bloodhound ever relax? He sticks so close he's beginning to grow on me ... like a fungus.

BRUNO ANTHONY: How do you do, sir? I, uh, I'd like to talk with you sometime, sir, and tell you about my idea for harnessing the life force. It'll make atomic power look like a horse and buggy. I'm already developing my faculty for seeing millions of miles. And Senator, can you imagine being able to smell a flower—on the planet Mars? I'd like to, uh, have lunch with you someday soon, sir, tell you more about it.

Clash by Night [1952]

JERRY D'AMATO: Earl? He's one of the smartest men I know. He's in the movie business.

MAE DOYLE D'AMATO: An actor?

JERRY D'AMATO: No, but I'll bet Earl could be if he wanted to. He works at the Bijou theatre, in the projection booth.

MAE DOYLE D'AMATO: That's your idea of being in the movie business?

JERRY D'AMATO: Running movies, what other business would you call it?

The Narrow Margin [1952]

DET. SGT. WALTER BROWN [TALKS ABOUT BRIBES]: I don't say I've never been tempted. Of course I've been tempted; I'm human like anybody else. To spend the rest of my time worrying when I'll be caught up with by some hoodlum holding a first mortgage on my life, payable on demand. … Naah. No kind of money worth that.

VINCENT YOST: We're ready to make a deal. You have her, we want her, how much? It's as simple as that.

DET. SGT. WALTER BROWN: You're under arrest.

VINCENT YOST: For what?

DET. SGT. WALTER BROWN: Attempted bribery.

VINCENT YOST: Bribery? Heh—you'd never make it stick. I'm a sales executive for the Midwest Equipment Company, Chicago. I've never even gotten as much as a parking ticket.

The Big Heat [1953]

KATIE BANNION: I've been thinking about Lieutenant Wilks.

DET. SGT. DAVE BANNION: That leaning tower of jelly.

City That Never Sleeps [1953]

SALLY "ANGEL FACE" CONNORS: When I first came to this town I was gonna be—oh, there were a lot of things I was gonna do. Become famous. But Chicago's the big melting pot, and I got melted, but good.

Pickup on South Street [1953]

SKIP McCOY: And I know you pinched me three times, got me convicted three times and made me a three-time loser. And I know you took an oath to put me away for life. Well you're trying awful hard with all this patriotic eye-wash, but get this: I didn't grift that film and you can't prove I did. And if I said I did, you'd slap that fourth rap across my teeth no matter what promises you made.

....

FBI AGENT: Do you know what treason means?

SKIP McCOY: Who cares?

....

CAPT. DAN TIGER: You'll always be a two-bit cannon and when they pick you up in the gutter dead, your hand'll be in a drunk's pocket.

Suddenly [1954]

JOHNNY BARON: Show me a guy who has feelings and I'll show you a sucker.

The Big Combo [1955]

MR. BROWN: Book me, small change.

....

CAPT. PETERSON: You can't tell a jury a man's guilty because "he's too innocent, it's unnatural."

....

CAPT. PETERSON: You're fightin' a swamp with a teaspoon.

The Big Knife [1955]

CHARLES CASTLE: I'm in the movie business, darling. I can't afford your acute attacks of integrity.

....

NAT DANZIGER: Pneumonia's at the door and we're talking about a headache.

....

STANLEY SHRINER HOFF: This man buries himself with his mouth.

She's under arrest, Mr. Brown. —LEONARD DIAMOND

What's the charge? —MR. BROWN

Homicide. —LEONARD DIAMOND

That's ridiculous, she wouldn't kill a fly. —MR. BROWN

She tried to kill herself. —LEONARD DIAMOND

Is that a crime? —MR. BROWN

It happens to be against two laws: God's and man's.

I'm booking her under the second. —LEONARD DIAMOND

The Big Combo 1955

PATTY BENEDICT: I want my gossip from the horse's mouth, not his tail.

Bob le Flambeur [1955] aka *Bob the Gambler, aka Fever Heat*

INSP. LEDRU: Criminal intent and attempt will get you five years. But with a good lawyer, you could knock it down to three. With an even better lawyer and no criminal intent, you could get an acquittal.

BOB MONTAGNÉ: And with a really top lawyer, I might sue for damages.

Kiss Me Deadly [1955] aka *Mickey Spillane's Kiss Me Deadly*

DR. G.E. SOBERIN: If you revive her, do you know what that will be? Resurrection, that's what it will be. And do you know what resurrection means? It means raise the dead.

And just who do you think you are that you think you can raise the dead?

....

VELDA: First, you find a little thread, the little thread leads you to a string, and the string leads you to a rope, and from the rope you hang by the neck.

The Naked Street [1955]

FINNEY: Nicky boy, you must have a rabbit's foot or something.

NICKY BRADNA: I got the whole bunny.

The Killing [1956]

JOHNNY CLAY: Now look, this friend of mine will be stopping by tomorrow and leaving a bundle for me. He's a cop.

....

JOE: A funny kind of a friend.

JOHNNY CLAY: He's a funny kind of a cop.

....

JOHNNY CLAY: You shot a horse. It isn't first-degree murder. In fact, it isn't even murder at all. In fact, I don't know what it is.

Slightly Scarlet [1956]

DET. LT./POLICE CHIEF DIETZ: You're a dreamer, Ben.

BEN GRACE: A man's only as big as his dream.

DET. LT./POLICE CHIEF DIETZ: They're going to pull you out of the river someday.

BEN GRACE: That's not part of the dream.

The Brothers Rico [1957]

JOHNNY RICO: Maybe I'm gonna die. You've got even bigger problems— you're gonna live.

Sweet Smell of Success [1957]

J.J. HUNSECKER: Mr. Falco, let it be said at once, is a man of forty faces, not one, none too pretty, and all deceptive.

....

SIDNEY FALCO: Watch me run a fifty-yard dash with my legs cut off.

....

J.J. HUNSECKER: Here's your head. What's your hurry?

Time Without Pity [1957]

DAVID GRAHAM: In common with quite a lot of other writers, I've been about to write for a very long time.

The Lineup [1958]

PHILIP DRESSLER: Well, it's unfortunate we have to meet under these awful circumstances, I know.

INSP. AL QUINE: We meet a lot of people under unpleasant circumstances, Mr. Dressler.

Touch of Evil [1958]

RAMON MIGUEL "MIKE" VARGAS: A policeman's job is only easy in a police state.

....

SGT. PETE MENZIES: You're a killer.

CAPT. HANK QUINLAN: Partly. I'm a cop.

Odds Against Tomorrow [1959]

BACCO: Tomorrow night at eight or I'll kill you and everything you own.

....

JOHNNY INGRAM: Yeah, yeah, I know. I got rid of the headache. Now I got cancer.

1961–1970

Blast of Silence [1961]

NARRATOR: The target's name is Troiano. You know the type: second-string syndicate boss with too much ambition. And a moustache to hide the fact he has lips like a woman. The kind of face you hate.

The Manchurian Candidate [1962]

RAYMOND SHAW: Twelve days of Christmas. One day of Christmas is loathsome enough.

....

CAPT./MAJ. BENNETT MARCO: Raymond Shaw is the kindest, bravest, warmest most wonderful human being I've ever known in my life.

Mélodie en Sous-Sol [1963] aka *Any Number Can Win*

MME. VERLOT: You'll end up killing your father and me—with grief.

FRANCIS VERLOT: At least they'll never find the murder weapon.

In Cold Blood [1967]

PERRY SMITH: It's true. Really true. We're on our way and we're never coming back. Never. No regrets.

DICK HICKOCK: For you. You're leaving nothing. What about my old man? And my mother? They'll still be there when my checks start bouncing.

PERRY SMITH: It's nice the way you think about your folks.

DICK HICKOCK: Yeah. I'm a real thoughtful bastard.

....

DICK HICKOCK: I got you figured for a natural born killer.

....

PERRY SMITH: I think maybe ... I'd like to apologize, but who to?

They Shoot Horses, Don't They? [1969]

SAILOR: Well, what I mean is, if you think about it, cattle ain't got it much better than us.

GLORIA: They got it better. There's always somebody feeding them.

....

ROCKY: You know something, Turkey? My old man never got out of the fourth grade. He knew people. He didn't know his ass from his elbow. You know what he was? He was a faith healer. I used to travel the circuit with him. I was the one he

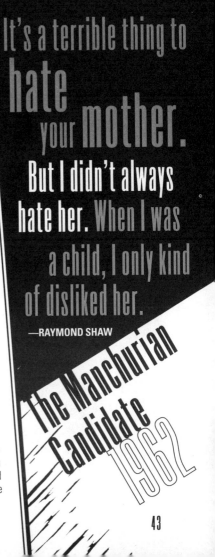

It's a terrible thing to **hate** your **mother.** But I didn't always hate her. When I was a child, I only kind of disliked her.

—RAYMOND SHAW

The Manchurian Candidate 1962

What do you want to **hack** for, Bickle?
—TAXI PERSONNEL OFFICER

I can't **sleep** nights.
—TRAVIS BICKLE

There's **porno** theaters for that.
—TAXI PERSONNEL OFFICER

Taxi Driver 1976

healed. I was the shill, get the crowd set up. "Walk, my boy. When I lay my hands on you, you will walk." You will walk. Sodden old bastard. He thought it was him they believed in. It was me.

1971–1980

Badlands [1973]

HOLLY SARGIS: At this moment, I didn't feel shame or fear, but just kind of blah, like when you're sitting there and all the water's run out of the bathtub.

The Friends of Eddie Coyle [1973]

EDDIE "FINGERS" COYLE: I should've known better than to trust a cop.

The Long Goodbye [1973]

PHILIP MARLOWE: It's okay with me.

Chinatown [1974]

NOAH CROSS [SERVES FISH FOR LUNCH]: I hope you don't mind. I believe they should be served with the head.

JAKE GITTES: Fine. As long as you don't serve the chicken that way.

The Conversation [1974]

HARRY CAUL: Why are you following me?

MARTIN STETT: I'm not following you. I'm looking for you. Big difference.

Farewell, My Lovely [1975]

BRUNETTE: We go back a long ways, to a time when you wanted to see me spanked.

PHILIP MARLOWE: I still do.

BRUNETTE: What for? All I do is run towns, elect judges and mayors, corrupt police, peddle dope, ice old ladies with pearls.

Taxi Driver [1976]

TRAVIS BICKLE: All the animals come out at night. Whores, skunk pussies, buggers, queens, fairies, dopers, junkies. Sick, venal. Someday a real rain will come and wash all the scum off the streets.

....

TRAVIS BICKLE: Loneliness has followed me my whole life, everywhere. In bars, in cars, sidewalks, stores, everywhere. There's no escape. I'm God's lonely man.

Straight Time [1978]

MAX DEMBO: I was a convict.

JENNEY MERCER: And how long did you hold that position?

MAX DEMBO: Approximately six years. No vacation.

Who'll Stop the Rain [1978]

JOHN CONVERSE: I've been waiting all my life to fuck up like this.

....

RAY HICKS: All my life I've been taking shit from inferior people. No more.

The Long Good Friday [1980]

HAROLD SHAND: The Mafia? I shit 'em.

1981–1990

Coup de Torchon [1981] aka *Clean Slate*

PRIEST: You never arrest anybody. How can they respect you? You've got to show folks you're brave, honest, and hardworking. Here, hold this.

The light that burns twice as bright burns half as long— and you have burned so very, very brightly, Roy. —DR. TYRELL

Blade Runner 1982

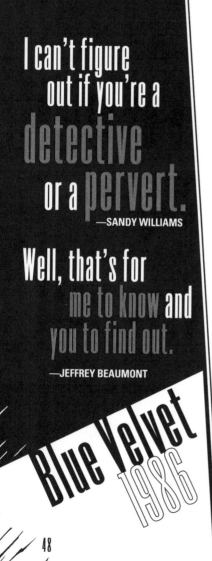

I can't figure out if you're a **detective** or a **pervert**.

—SANDY WILLIAMS

Well, that's for **me to know** and **you to find out**.

—JEFFREY BEAUMONT

Blue Velvet 1986

48

[LUCIEN HOLDS DOWN A STATUE OF CHRIST FOR THE PRIEST WHILE HE NAILS IT TO A CROSS.]

LUCIEN CORDIER: I can't.

PRIEST: Why not?

LUCIEN CORDIER: First, because I'm not brave, honest, and hardworking. And second, I don't think my chiefs want me to be.

PRIEST: What are you talking about?

LUCIEN CORDIER: Well, they wouldn't have picked me otherwise.

....

LUCIEN CORDIER: Doing nothing is my job. I'm paid for it.

....

ROSE [SHE HAS MURDERED HUGUETTE AND NONO]: You saw everything?

LUCIEN CORDIER: Let's say I heard everything. It's all the same.

ROSE: And you did nothing?

LUCIEN CORDIER: Why should I? Coffee?

ROSE: Why … to stop me.

LUCIEN CORDIER: It wasn't up to me to stop you. It was up to you, to Huguette, Nono, Marcaillou. I might lead you into temptation, but is this a good enough reason not to stop? I just help people to reveal their real nature. It's a dirty job, Rose. And you might very well say I deserve all the dirty pleasure I get out of it.

ROSE: Aren't you ashamed of speaking like this?

LUCIEN CORDIER: That's yet another aspect of my business, enjoying other people's misery.

Cutter's Way [1981]

ALEX CUTTER: You think we could mug a horse?

....

ALEX CUTTER: You know, the routine grind drives me to drink. Tragedy I take straight.

True Confessions [1981]

JACK AMSTERDAM: Hey, the Cardinal ever go to the track? Maybe he'll be my guest one day. I'll give him a couple of tips.

DAN T. CAMPION: Jack gives you a tip, you can bet the Sistine Chapel on it.

....

DAN T. CAMPION: Looks like a leprechaun, thinks like an Arab.

Blade Runner [1982]

LEON: Wake up. Time to die.

....

ROY BATTY: It's not an easy thing to meet your maker.

DR. TYRELL: What could he do for you?

ROY BATTY: Can the maker repair what he makes?

....

ROY BATTY: I want more life, fucker.

Blood Simple [1984]

JULIAN MARTY: I got a job for you.

PVT. DET. LOREN VISSER: Uh, well, if the pay's right, and it's legal, I'll do it.

JULIAN MARTY: It's not strictly legal.

PVT. DET. LOREN VISSER: Well, if the pay's right, I'll do it.

Manhunter [1986]

WILL GRAHAM: I know that I'm not smarter than you.

DR. HANNIBAL LECKTOR: Then how did you catch me?

WILL GRAHAM: You had disadvantages.

DR. HANNIBAL LECKTOR: What disadvantages?

WILL GRAHAM: You're insane.

....

DR. HANNIBAL LECKTOR: The reason you caught me is, we're just alike. You want the scent, smell yourself.

Miami Blues [1990]

SGT. HOKE MOSELEY: Your turn to notify next of kin.

SGT. BILL HENDERSON: No way. I did the fat lady that sat on her kid. That's good for two.

....

FREDERICK J. FRENGER, JR.: I used to be in prison.

SUSIE WAGGONER: What'd you do to get there?

FREDERICK J. FRENGER, JR.: I used to rob people who robbed people.

SUSIE WAGGONER: Sort of like Robin Hood?

FREDERICK J. FRENGER, JR.: Yeah, except I didn't give the money to the poor people.

The Two Jakes [1990]

JAKE GITTES: I suppose it's fair to say that infidelity made me what I am today.

....

JAKE GITTES: Frankly, if I waited for an honest client, I'd be sitting around until Rocky Graziano played Rachmaninoff at the Hollywood Bowl.

You shoot me in a dream, you'd better wake up and apologize.

—MR. WHITE

Reservoir Dogs 1992

I want you to go in that bag
and hand me my wallet.
—JULES WINNFIELD

Which one is it?
—PUMPKIN/RINGO

It's the one that says
"Bad Motherfucker."
—JULES WINNFIELD

Pulp Fiction 1994

JAKE GITTES: What I do for a living may not be very reputable. But I am. In this town I'm the leper with the most fingers.

JAKE GITTES: Most cops' ethics are a little like the cars they drive—black and white.

EARL RAWLEY: I prefer matches, thank you. I love the smell of sulfur.

JAKE GITTES: You're crazy, Mickey.

MICKEY NICE: That may be, but do you know a better way to stay healthy?

1991–2000

Reservoir Dogs [1992]

MR. PINK: You kill anybody?

MR. WHITE: A few cops.

MR. PINK: No real people?

MR. WHITE: Just cops.

MR. PINK: Somebody's sticking a red-hot poker up our ass, and I want to know whose name is on the handle.

White Sands [1992]

BERT GIBSON: Ease off. You're as persistent as a dog with two dicks.

Romeo Is Bleeding [1993]

JACK GRIMALDI: So you're the big hoodlum? Personally, I don't see it.

MONA DEMARKOV: Keep looking.

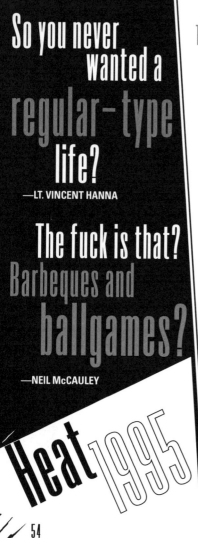

So you never
wanted a
**regular-type
life?**
—LT. VINCENT HANNA

The fuck is that?
Barbeques and
ballgames?
—NEIL McCAULEY

Heat 1995

54

True Romance [1993]

VINCENZO COCCOTTI: You know who I am, Mr. Worley?

CLIFFORD WORLEY: I give up. Who are you?

VINCENZO COCCOTTI: The Anti-Christ. You get me in a vendetta kind of mood, you tell the angels in heaven you never seen evil so singularly personified as you did in the face of the man who killed you. My name is Vincent Coccotti. I work as counsel for Mr. Blue Lou Boyle, the man your son stole from.

....

ELLIOT BLITZER: Hi. How are you? My name's Elliot and I'm with the Cub Scouts of America. We're selling uncut cocaine to get to the jamboree.

....

CODY NICHOLSON [HARANGUES ELLIOT]: Hey, you got caught. It's all fun and fuckin' games 'til you get caught. But now we got ya, OK, Mr. Elliot fucking actor, you just made the big time.

NICKY DIMES: You're no longer an extra ...

CODY NICHOLSON: ... or a bit player ...

NICKY DIMES: ... or a supporting actor ...

CODY NICHOLSON: ... you're a fucking star. You're a fucking star. And you are going to be playing your one-man show nightly for the next two fucking years for a captive audience. And listen to this, you get out in a few years, you meet some old lady, you'll get married, and you'll be so understanding to your wife's needs because you'll know what it feels like to be a woman.

NICKY DIMES: Of course, you'll only want to fuck her in the ass because that pussy just won't be tight enough for you anymore.

CODY NICHOLSON: Good point, detective.

....

DREXL SPIVEY: Now I know I'm pretty, but I ain't as pretty as a couple of titties.

Shallow Grave [1994]

ALEX LAW: I'd like to ask you about your hobbies. . . . Now when you sacrifice a goat and you rip its heart out with your bare hands, do you then summon hellfire? Or do you just send out for a pizza?

....

DET. INSP. McCALL: But in your work you must meet lots of different people every day. New people, new faces, no?

JULIET MILLER: Yes.

DET. INSP. McCALL: What do you recognize most, names or faces?

JULIET MILLER: Diseases.

DET. INSP. McCALL: Like recognizing criminals by their crimes.

Clockers [1995]

DET. ROCCO KLEIN [YANKS TARP OFF DARYL ADAMS' CORPSE]: Boys, Daryl Adams. Daryl Adams, the boys.

....

DET. LARRY MAZILLA [LOOKS AT SLUG STUCK IN DARYL ADAMS' MOUTH]: Marvello the magician. Catch a bullet with his teeth.

CHORUS OF OTHER DETECTIVES: What a catch. What a smile.

DET. ROCCO KLEIN: Darryl, you've outdone Willie Mays. You got my vote for MVP.

DET. LARRY MAZILLA: Another stain on the sidewalk, huh?

....

COP: They should blow these projects to Timbuktu.

DET. LARRY MAZILLA: Why bother? They kill themselves anyway. One of those self-cleaning ovens.

RODNEY LITTLE: God created anything better than crack cocaine he kept that shit for hisself. I mean that shit is like truth serum, it will truly expose who you are. You happen to be a lowlife rat bastard motherfucker, who would sell off his newborn for a suck off that glass dick, crack will bring it right on in the light. I don't care if you black, white, Chinese, rich, poor, you take that first hit, you on a mission and that mission will never end. Even when the house, money, loved ones are gone, and they send you to the joint, you still going to try to cop it.

RODNEY LITTLE: Only time it ends, Strike, that mission, is when you six feet under.

Heat [1995]

NEIL MCCAULEY: It is what it is. It's that or we better go do something else, pal.

LT. VINCENT HANNA: I don't know how to do anything else.

NEIL McCAULEY: Neither do I.

LT. VINCENT HANNA: I don't much want too, either.

NEIL McCAULEY: Neither do I.

NEIL MCCAULEY: Guy told me one time, don't let yourself get attached to anything you are not willing to walk out on in thirty seconds flat if you feel the heat around the corner.

LT. VINCENT HANNA: You know, we're sitting here, you and I, like a couple of regular fellows. You do what you do, I do what I gotta do. And now that we've been face to face, if I'm there and I gotta put you away, I won't like it. But I'll tell you, if it's between you and some poor bastard whose wife you're gonna turn into a widow, brother, you are going down.

NEIL McCAULEY: There's a flip side to that coin. What if you do got me boxed in and I gotta have to put you down? 'Cause no matter what, you will not get in my way. We've been face to face, yeah. But I will not hesitate, not for a second.

NEIL McCAULEY: You see me doing thrill-seeker liquor store holdups with a "Born to Lose" tattoo on my chest?

You know, this isn't going to have a happy ending.

—DET. LT. WILLIAM SOMERSET

Se7en 1995

I don't trust the **jury** system, the **phone** company or the **Israeli** government.

—VICTOR SPANSKY

Blood and Wine 1996

NEIL McCAULEY [TALKS ON PHONE]: Forget the money.

ROGER VAN ZANT: It's a lot of money. What are you doing? What do you mean, forget the money?

NEIL McCAULEY: What am I doing? I'm talking to an empty telephone.

ROGER VAN ZANT: I don't understand.

NEIL McCAULEY: 'Cause there is a dead man on the other end of this fuckin' line.

Kiss of Death [1995]

RONNIE GANNON: You know what your problem is? You're a liberal.

Se7en [1995]

DET. DAVID MILLS: I've been trying to figure something in my head, and maybe you can help me out, yeah? When a person is insane, as you clearly are, do you know that you're insane? Maybe you're just sitting around, reading *Guns and Ammo,* masturbating in your own feces, do you just stop and go, "Wow. It is amazing how fucking crazy I really am"? Yeah? Do you guys do that?

JOHN DOE: It's more comfortable for you to label me as insane.

DET. DAVID MILLS: It's very comfortable.

DR. BEARDSLEY: He's experienced about as much pain and suffering as anyone I've encountered, give or take, and he still has hell to look forward to.

DET. DAVID MILLS: C'mon, he's insane. Look. Right now he's probably dancing around in his grandma's panties, yeah, rubbing himself in peanut butter.

DET. LT. WILLIAM SOMERSET: This guy is methodical, exacting, and worst of all, patient.

DET. DAVID MILLS: He's a nut-bag. Just because the … the fucker's got a library card doesn't make him Yoda.

DET. DAVID MILLS: Wait a minute, I thought all you did was kill innocent people.

JOHN DOE: Innocent? Is that supposed to be funny? An obese man, a disgusting man who could barely stand up; a man if you saw him on the street, you'd point him out to your friends so that they could join you in mocking him; a man, who if you saw him while you were eating, you wouldn't be able to finish your meal. And after him, I picked the lawyer and you both must have secretly been thanking me for that one.

DET. DAVID MILLS: You're no messiah. You're a … you're a movie of the week. You're a fucking T-shirt, at best.

JOHN DOE: Don't ask me to pity those people. I don't mourn them any more than I do the thousands that died at Sodom and Gomorrah.

DET. LT. WILLIAM SOMERSET: If John Doe's head splits open and a UFO should fly out, I want you to have expected it.

JOHN DOE: We see a deadly sin on every street corner, in every home, and we tolerate it. We tolerate it because it's common, it's trivial. We tolerate it morning, noon, and night. Well, not anymore. I'm setting the example. And what I've done is going to be puzzled over, and studied, and followed … forever.

Strange Days [1995]

LENNY NERO: I am your main connection to the switchboard of the soul. I'm the magic man, the Santa Claus of the subconscious.

"It's Christmas Eve in the City of Angels
and while decent citizens sleep
the sleep of the righteous,
hopheads prowl for marijuana,
not knowing that a man is coming
to stop them.
Celebrity crimestopper Jack Vincennes,
scourge of grasshoppers
and dope fiends everywhere.
Ya like it, Jackie-Boy?" —SID HUDGENS

Yeah. Subtle. —SGT. JACK VINCENNES

L.A. Confidential 1997

The Usual Suspects [1995]

VERBAL KINT: The greatest trick the Devil ever pulled was convincing the world he didn't exist.

Fargo [1996]

JERRY LUNDEGAARD: Now we had a deal here. A deal's a deal.

CARL SHOWALTER: Is it, Jerry? Why don't you ask those three poor souls in Brainerd if a deal's a deal. Go ahead, ask them.

JERRY LUNDEGAARD: The heck do ya mean?

CARL SHOWALTER: "The heck da ya mean?"

....

POLICE CHIEF MARGE GUNDERSON: I'm not sure I agree with you a hundred percent on your police work there, Lou.

....

GAEAR GRIMSRUD: You are a smooth smoothie, you know.

....

POLICE CHIEF MARGE GUNDERSON: Oh, you betcha, ya.

City of Industry [1997]

CATHI ROSE: Why don't you call the police?

ROY EGAN: I'm my own police.

....

CATHI ROSE: The Skip I know doesn't have friends, just people he fucks over.

L.A. Confidential [1997]

SGT. JACK VINCENNES: Oh, lookee here, the great jerk-off case of 1953.

....

OFFICER: What took you, Stensland?

SGT. RICHARD ALEX "DICK" STENSLAND: My partner stopped to help a damsel in distress. He's got his priorities all screwed up.

PIERCE PATCHETT: I use girls that look like movie stars. Sometimes I employ a plastic surgeon. When the work had been done, that's when you saw us.

OFFICER WENDELL "BUD" WHITE: That's why her mother couldn't I.D. her. Jesus fucking Christ.

PIERCE PATCHETT: No, Mr. White. Pierce Morehouse Patchett.

....

CAPT. DUDLEY SMITH: Edmund, you're a political animal. You have the eye for human weakness, but not the stomach.

SGT. EDMUND JENNINGS EXLEY: You're wrong, sir.

CAPT. DUDLEY SMITH: Would you be willing to plant corroborative evidence on a suspect you knew to be guilty, in order to ensure an indictment?

SGT. EDMUND JENNINGS EXLEY: Dudley, we've been over this.

CAPT. DUDLEY SMITH: Yes or no, Edmund?

SGT. EDMUND JENNINGS EXLEY: No.

CAPT. DUDLEY SMITH: Would you be willing to beat a confession out of a suspect you knew to be guilty?

SGT. EDMUND JENNINGS EXLEY: No.

CAPT. DUDLEY SMITH: Would you be willing to shoot a hardened criminal in the back, in order to offset the chance that some lawyer ...

SGT. EDMUND JENNINGS EXLEY: No.

CAPT. DUDLEY SMITH: Then, for the love of God, don't be a detective. Stick to assignments where you don't have make those kind of choices.

....

CAPT. DUDLEY SMITH: I wouldn't trade places with Edmund Exley right now for all the whisky in Ireland.

....

CAPT. DUDLEY SMITH: You'll do as I say, and ask no questions. Do you follow my drift?

OFFICER WENDELL "BUD" WHITE: In Technicolor, sir.

What do you do for recreation?
—MAUDE LEBOWSKI

Oh, the usual. **Bowl.**
Drive around.
The occasional acid flashback.
—THE DUDE

The Big Lebowski
1998

The Big Lebowski [1998]

THE DUDE: Do you see a wedding ring on my finger? Does this place look like I'm fucking married? The toilet seat's up, man.

....

THE DUDE: I could be sitting here with just pee stains on my rug.

....

THE DUDE: You know, this is a very complicated case, Maude. Lot of ins, lot of outs. Uh, you know, fortunately, I'm adhering to a pretty strict, uh, drug, uh, regimen to keep my mind, you know, uh, limber.

....

THE DUDE: It's like Lenin said … you look for the person who will benefit, and, uh, uh … you know … uh …

DONNY: I am the walrus.

THE DUDE: You know, you'll, uh … uh … you know what I'm trying to say …

DONNY: I am the walrus.

WALTER SOBCHAK: That fucking bitch.

DONNY: I am the walrus.

WALTER SOBCHAK: Shut the fuck up, Donny. V.I. Lenin. Vladimir Ilyich Ulyanov.

Dark City [1998]

DR. DANIEL SCHREBER: First came darkness, then came the strangers.

Rounders [1998]

LESTER "WORM" MURPHY: I mean, he sees all the angles but he doesn't have the balls to play one.

....

MIKE McDERMOTT: We're not playing together, but then again we're not playing against each other, either. It's like the Nature Channel—you don't see piranha eating each other, do you?

Well, whatever you do, however terrible, however hurtful, it all makes sense, doesn't it, in your head? You never meet anybody who thinks they're a bad person.

—TOM RIPLEY

The Talented Mr. Ripley 1999

Must be tough living your life according to a couple of scraps of paper. Mix your laundry list with your grocery list and you'll end up eating your underwear for breakfast. —NATALIE

Memento 2001

Twilight [1998]

RAYMOND HOPE: Jack Ames couldn't get blood out of a sock with a washing machine and a gallon of Clorox. Me, I can get blood out of a sock.

....

RAYMOND HOPE: Don't you ever get tired of the beautiful people? Doesn't it ever bother you that the Jacks and the Catherines of this world can do as they please because it's always guys like you and me who'll clean up after them?

....

JACK AMES: Fuck you.

HARRY ROSS: Just me? Not the horse I rode in on?

JACK AMES: Him too.

8MM [1999]

DINO VELVET: Mr. Longdale, if there's no honor among perverts and pornographers, the whole fucking business will fall apart.

The Talented Mr. Ripley [1999]

DICKIE GREENLEAF: Everybody should have one talent. What's yours?

TOM RIPLEY: Forging signatures, telling lies, and impersonating practically anybody.

Nueve Reinas [2000] aka *Nine Queens*

JUAN: What did you say when asked what you wanted to be?

MARCOS: Left wing.

JUAN: I wanted to be an accomplice.

The Way of the Gun [2000]

HALE CHIDDUCK: I would never ask you to trust me. It's the cry of a guilty soul.

2001–2005

Memento [2001]

LEONARD SHELBY: These tracks are only a few days old.

JOHN EDWARD "TEDDY" GAMMELL: Tracks? What are you, Pocahontas?

....

NATALIE: What's the last thing that you do remember?

LEONARD SHELBY: My wife.

NATALIE: That's sweet.

LEONARD SHELBY: Dying.

Scotland, PA [2001]

JOE "MAC" McBETH: I hate to break it to ya, Lieutenant, but this is not an episode of Columbo. All right? I'm not gonna break down, hand you the gun, and get waltzed out of here between a couple of good-looking cops with my head bowed down.

25th Hour [2002]

JAKOB ELINSKY: What do we say to him?

FRANK XAVIER SLAUGHTERY: We say nothin'. He's going to hell for seven years. What am I gonna do, wish him luck?

....

MONTY BROGAN: Fuck this whole city and everyone in it, from the row houses of Astoria to the penthouses on Park Avenue, from the projects in the Bronx to the lofts in Soho, from the tenements in Alphabet City to the brownstones in Park Slope to the split-levels in Staten Island. Let an earthquake crumble it. Let the fires rage. Let it burn to fucking ash and then let the waters rise and submerge this whole rat-infested place. No, no, fuck you Montgomery Brogan. You had it all and you threw it away, you dumb fuck.

Dark Blue [2002]

JACK VAN METER: I am a performer of unpleasant tasks so that the majority of people are free to perform pleasant ones.

ELDON PERRY: The only reason this goddamn city's here is because they made it possible. They built it with bullets.

SALLY PERRY: You care more about the people you hate.

Insomnia [2002]

DET. ELLIE BURR: A good cop can't sleep because a piece of the puzzle's missing. And a bad cop can't sleep because his conscience won't let him.

DET. WILL DORMER: It's all about small stuff. You know, small lies, small mistakes. People give themselves away, same in misdemeanors as they do in murder cases.

DET. WILL DORMER: You don't get it, do you, Finch? You're my job. You're what I'm paid to do. You're about as mysterious to me as a blocked toilet is to a fucking plumber. Reasons for doing what you did? Who gives a fuck?

Narc [2002]

DET. SGT. NICK TELLIS: My duty assignment was solely undercover narcotic work. Do you have any idea what that entails?

You gotta be **heartless** in my line of work.

—ELDON PERRY

Dark Blue 2002

LIZ DETMER: I have a general idea, yeah.

DET. SGT. NICK TELLIS: OK. Well, then, generally speaking, Ms. Detmer, you don't know what the fuck you're talking about.

The Quiet American [2002]

THOMAS FOWLER: And there was Alden Pyle. The face with no history, no problems. The face we all had once.

Ripley's Game [2002]

JONATHAN TREVANNY: Who are you?

TOM RIPLEY: I'm a creation. I'm a gifted improviser. I lack your conscience, and when I was young that troubled me. It no longer does.

The Salton Sea [2002]

DANNY PARKER: Tweakers, lokers, slammers coming and going, swearing eternal allegiance and undying love for one another, only to wake up after the binge and realize you wouldn't walk across the street to piss on one of them if their head was on fire.

....

KUJO: My wife's pimp knows a guy who works at Cedars Sinai medical lab, and he's gonna be making a very special delivery a week from this Friday.

JIMMY THE FINN: Is it drugs?

KUJO: Better than drugs. Bob Hope's stool specimen. We're gonna boost it.

....

JIMMY THE FINN: They say he hasn't slept in like over a year.

DANNY PARKER: Bullshit.

JIMMY THE FINN: Naw, it's true. I've never seen him sleep. Seriously.

DANNY PARKER: Have you ever seen Queen Elizabeth sleep?

JIMMY THE FINN: No. Why, is she a tweaker?

Confidence [2003]

WINSTON KING: Sometimes, Jake, style can get you killed.

JAKE VIG: Hey, what do you say you get the ADD under control, you look me in the eye when I talk to you?

TRAVIS: You know who I am, Jake?
JAKE VIG: Uh, the Anti-Christ?

The Cooler [2003]

SHELLY KAPLOW: Lootz is kryptonite on a stick.

Mystic River [2003]

ANNABETH MARKUM: Because it's like I told the girls. Their daddy is a king. And a king knows what to do and does it.

Xun Qiang [2003]
aka *The Missing Gun*

MA SHAN: I didn't lose my gun. It's missing.

Sin City [2005]

DWIGHT: Most people think Marv is crazy. He just had the rotten luck of being born in the wrong century. He'd be right at home on some ancient battlefield swinging a mace into somebody's face. Or in a Roman arena taking a sword to other gladiators like him.

Hell, I'll die laughing if I know I've done this one thing right. —MARV

Sin City 2005

You're a *bitter* little lady.
—JOHN MULLER/DR. VICTOR EMIL BARTOK

It's a
bitter
little world.
—EVELYN HAHN

Hollow Triumph 1948

CHAPTER TWO

The Dames and the Mugs

1941–1950

High Sierra [1941]

ROY "MAD DOG" EARLE: I wouldn't give you two cents for a dame without a temper.

The Maltese Falcon [1941]

BRIGID O'SHAUGHNESSY: I haven't lived a good life. I've been bad, worse than you could know.

SAM SPADE: You know, that's good, because if you actually were as innocent as you pretend to be, we'd never get anywhere.

SAM SPADE: I don't care who loves who. I won't play the sap for you.

SAM SPADE: Chances are you'll get off with life. That means if you're a good girl, you'll be out in twenty years. I'll be waiting for you. If they hang you … I'll always remember you.

The Shanghai Gesture [1941]

DR. OMAR: Allah be praised for always providing new women.

I Wake Up Screaming [1942]

ROBIN RAY: Women are all alike.

LARRY EVANS: For Pete's sake, what difference does that make? You're got to have them. They're standard equipment.

This Gun for Hire [1942]

WILLARD GATES: I want to know all about you.

ELLEN GRAHAM: That's a big little word, "all."

WILLARD GATES: Well, practically all.

Shadow of a Doubt [1943]

UNCLE CHARLIE: The cities are full of women, middle-aged widows, husbands, dead husbands who've spent their lives making fortunes, working and working. And then they die and leave their money to their wives, their silly wives. And what do the wives do, these useless women? You see them in the hotels, the best hotels, every day by the thousands, drinking the money, eating the money, losing the money at bridge, playing all day and all night, smelling of money, proud of their jewelry but of nothing else, horrible, faded, fat, greedy women.

UNCLE CHARLIE: Are they human or are they fat, wheezing animals, hmm? And what happens to animals when they get too fat and too old?

Christmas Holiday [1944]

SIMON FENIMORE: Bad boy meets good girl. Damage estimated at $10,000.

Double Indemnity [1944]

WALTER NEFF: I killed him for money and for a woman. I didn't get the money. And I didn't get the woman.

....

WALTER NEFF: You'll be here, too?

PHYLLIS DIETRICHSON: I guess so. I usually am.

WALTER NEFF: Same chair, same perfume, same anklet?

PHYLLIS DIETRICHSON: I wonder if I know what you mean.

WALTER NEFF: I wonder if you wonder.

....

WALTER NEFF: It's just like the first time I came here, isn't it? We were talking about automobile insurance, only you were thinking about murder. And I was thinking about that anklet.

Laura [1944]

WALDO LYDECKER: I shall never forget the weekend Laura died. A silver sun burned through the sky like a huge magnifying glass. It was the hottest Sunday in my recollection. I felt as if I were the only human being left in New York. ... I had just begun Laura's story when another of those detectives came to see me. I had him wait.

I saw her **first.** Let's not forget that. —DR. OMAR

The Shanghai Gesture 1941

I must say,
for a charming, intelligent girl,
you certainly surrounded
yourself with a
remarkable collection
of dopes.

—DET. LT. MARK McPHERSON

Laura 1944

DET. LT. MARK McPHERSON: Yeah, dames are always pulling a switch on you.

WALDO LYDECKER: Young woman, either you have been raised in some incredibly rustic community where good manners are unknown, or you suffer from the common feminine illusion that the mere fact of being a woman exempts you from the rules of civilized conduct. Possibly both.

WALDO LYDECKER: Ever know a woman who wasn't a doll or a dame?

DET. LT. MARK McPHERSON: Yeah, one. But she kept walking me past furniture windows to look at the parlor suites.

DET. LT. MARK McPHERSON: When a dame gets killed, she doesn't worry about how she looks.

Murder, My Sweet [1944]

MOOSE MALLOY: She was cute as lace pants.

PHILIP MARLOWE: She was a charming middle-aged lady with a face like a bucket of mud. I gave her a drink. She was a gal who'd take a drink, if she had to knock you down to get the bottle.

Phantom Lady [1944]

CLIFF MILBURN: You like jive?

CAROL "KANSAS" RICHMAN: You bet. I'm a hep kitten.

SCOTT HENDERSON: Oh, by the way, my name is …

ANN TERRY: Oh, no, no names, no addresses. Just companions for the evening …

Conflict [1945]

KATHERINE MASON: It's funny how virtuous a man can be when he's vulnerable.

DR. MARK HAMILTON: But you see, marriage is a very tricky business. People have impulses, compulsions, and drives, let us say, toward escape, and escape from loneliness. They seek that escape in the companionship of someone else. And, lo, just when they think they've achieved it, they finally put on their own handcuffs.

EVELYN TURNER: I beg your pardon, Dr. Hamilton. Love doesn't always cause unhappiness and trouble. It's been man's inspiration for centuries. Why, it's been the basis of some of the greatest stories ever written. Look at Romeo and Juliet. Antony and Cleopatra. Abelard and Heloise.

RICHARD MASON: Yes, but look what happened to them.

Detour [1945]

CHARLES HASKELL, JR.: I was tussling with the most dangerous animal in the world: A woman.

VERA: Not only don't you have any scruples, you don't have any brains.

VERA: Shut up, you're making noises like a husband.

Mildred Pierce [1945]

MILDRED PIERCE: I know you romantic guys. One crack about the beautiful moon and you're off to the races.

WALLY FAY: You know, I wouldn't drop dead at the idea of marrying you.

Scarlet Street [1945]

ADELE CROSS: Next thing you'll be painting women without clothes.
CHRISTOPHER CROSS: I never saw a woman without any clothes.
ADELE CROSS: I should hope not.

KITTY MARCH: If he were mean or vicious or if he'd bawl me out or something, I'd like him better.

JOHNNY PRINCE: I don't know what you told Janeway, but you got him eatin' right out of your hand.

KITTY MARCH: It won't stop with lunch.

KITTY MARCH: How can a man be so dumb. ... I've been waiting to laugh in your face ever since I met you. You're old and ugly and I'm sick of you. Sick, sick, sick.

Spellbound [1945]

JOHN BALLANTINE/JOHN BROWN/DR. ANTHONY EDWARDES: Now, this honeymoon is complicated enough without your dragging medical ethics into it.

DR. ALEX BRULOV: Women make the best psychoanalysts until they fall in love. After that they make the best patients.

The Big Sleep [1946]

CARMEN STERNWOOD: You're not very tall are you?

PHILIP MARLOWE: Well, I, uh, I try to be.

VIVIAN STERNWOOD RUTLEDGE: Well, speaking of horses, I like to play them myself. But I like to see them work out a little first, see if they're front-runners or come-from-behind, find out what their hole card is. What makes them run.

PHILIP MARLOWE: Find out mine?

VIVIAN STERNWOOD RUTLEDGE: I think so.

Friendship's much more lasting than love.

—MILDRED PIERCE

Yeah, but it isn't as entertaining.

—WALLY FAY

Mildred Pierce 1945

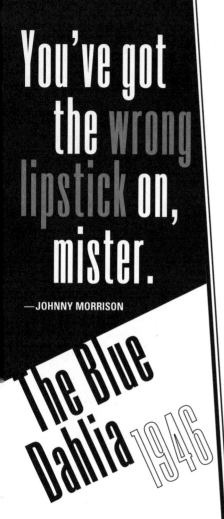

You've got the wrong lipstick on, mister.

—JOHNNY MORRISON

The Blue Dahlia 1946

PHILIP MARLOWE: Go ahead.

VIVIAN STERNWOOD RUTLEDGE: I'd say you don't like to be rated. You like to get out in front, open up a lead, take a little breather in the backstretch, and then come home free.

PHILIP MARLOWE: You don't like to be rated yourself.

VIVIAN STERNWOOD RUTLEDGE: I haven't met anyone yet that can do it. Any suggestions?

PHILIP MARLOWE: Well, I can't tell 'til I've seen you over a distance of ground. You've got a touch of class, but, uh … I don't know how … how far you can go.

VIVIAN STERNWOOD RUTLEDGE: A lot depends on who's in the saddle.

PHILIP MARLOWE: Good morning.

VIVIAN STERNWOOD RUTLEDGE: So you do get up. I was beginning to think perhaps you worked in bed like Marcel Proust.

PHILIP MARLOWE: Who's he?

VIVIAN STERNWOOD RUTLEDGE: You wouldn't know him, French writer.

PHILIP MARLOWE: Come into my boudoir.

PHILIP MARLOWE: There's one thing I can't figure out.

VIVIAN STERNWOOD RUTLEDGE: What makes me run?

PHILIP MARLOWE: Uh-huh.

VIVIAN STERNWOOD RUTLEDGE: I'll give you a little hint. Sugar won't work. It's been tried.

It's a Bitter Little World

PHILIP MARLOWE: Did I hurt you much, sugar?

AGNES: You and every other man I've ever met.

....

FEMALE BOOKSTORE CLERK: You begin to interest me ... vaguely.

....

LIBRARIAN: You know, you don't look like a man who'd be interested in first editions.

PHILIP MARLOWE: I collect blondes and bottles, too.

....

PHILIP MARLOWE: What's wrong with you?

VIVIAN STERNWOOD RUTLEDGE: Nothing you can't fix.

Black Angel [1946]

CATHERINE BENNETT: I seem to have said all the wrong things.

JOE: Yeah, most women do.

The Blue Dahlia [1946]

HELEN MORRISON: I take all the drinks I like, any time, any place. I go where I want to with anybody I want. I just happen to be that kind of a girl.

The Chase [1946]

EDDIE ROMAN: Rhonda doesn't travel much.

EMMERICH JOHNSON: Oh, doctor's orders?

EDDIE ROMAN: No, mine.

Gilda [1946]

JOHNNY FARRELL: Statistics show that there are more women in the world than anything else. Except insects.

....

JOHNNY FARRELL: I hated her so I couldn't get her out of my mind for a minute.

The Dames and the Mugs

JOHNNY FARRELL: Pardon me, but your husband is showing.

The Killers [1946]

KITTY COLLINS: I'm poison, Swede, to myself and everybody around me.

Nocturne [1946]

SUSAN FLANDERS: He was a lady-killer, but don't get any ideas—I ain't no lady.

Notorious [1946]

ALICIA: Well, did you hear that? I'm practically on the wagon, that's quite a change.

DEVLIN: It's a phase.

ALICIA: You don't think a woman can change?

DEVLIN: Sure, change is fun, for a while.

ALICIA: This is a very strange love affair.

DEVLIN: Why?

ALICIA: Maybe the fact that you don't love me.

ALICIA: There's nothing like a love song to give you a good laugh.

ALICIA: Say it again, it keeps me awake.

DEVLIN: I love you.

ALICIA [DRIVING UNDER THE INFLUENCE]: This fog gets to me.

DEVLIN: It's your hair in your eyes.

DEVLIN: Don't you need a coat?

ALICIA: You'll do.

Doesn't it bother you at all
that you're married?

—JOHNNY FARREEL

What I want to know is,
does it bother you?

—GILDA

Gilda 1946

The Postman Always Rings Twice [1946]

FRANK CHAMBERS: Stealing a man's wife, that's nothing. But stealing his car, that's larceny.

....

FRANK CHAMBERS: I can sell anything to anybody.
CORA SMITH: That's what you think.

....

FRANK CHAMBERS: I've been waiting a long time for that kiss.
CORA SMITH: When we get home, Frank, then there'll be kisses. Kisses with dreams in them. Kisses that come from life, not death.

The Spiral Staircase [1946]

MRS. OATES: Here, where's my brandy?
MR. OATES: I finished it for your own good.

Undercurrent [1946]

LUCY: Roses don't show respect—roses show intentions.

Body and Soul [1947]

ALICE: Don't romance me, Quinn. You're getting old.
QUINN: You could use a new paint job yourself.

....

ALICE: What have I got to lose?
CHARLEY DAVIS: What have you got to win?

Born to Kill [1947]

HELEN TRENT: There's a kind of depravity in you, Sam.

Crossfire [1947]

GINNY TREMAINE: OK, where were you when he needed you? Maybe you were someplace having beautiful thoughts. Well, I wasn't. I was in a stinkin' gin mill, where all he had to do to see me was walk in, sit down at the table and buy me a drink.

Dark Passage [1947]

VINCENT PARRY: Maybe some day she'll get run over, or something.

GEORGE FELLSINGER: That's what I pray for every night.

Dead Reckoning [1947]

CAPT. WARREN "RIP" MURDOCK: Didn't I tell you all females are all the same with their faces washed?

The Devil Thumbs a Ride [1947]

AGNES: I'd eat a cow if somebody took the horns off.

....

AGNES [MARVELS AT THE NOVEL SHE'S READING]: Hey, by tomorrow will I have an improved mind. Can this boy write. Say, who is this Balzac anyhow?

FURGIE: Get your clothes on and come out here.

The Lady From Shanghai [1947]

MICHAEL O'HARA: Personally, I don't like a girlfriend to have a husband. If she'll fool a husband, I figure she'll fool me.

....

ARTHUR BANNISTER: You know, for a smart girl, you make a lot of mistakes. You should have let me live. You're going to need a good lawyer.

Lady in the Lake [1947]

ADRIENNE FROMSETT: Tell me, Mr. Marlowe, you always fall in love with all your clients?

PHILIP MARLOW: Only the ones in skirts.

Don't you see you've only me to make deals with now?

—KATHIE MOFFAT

Build my gallows high, baby.

—JEFF BAILEY/JEFF MARKHAM

Out of the Past
1947

PHILIP MARLOWE: When it concerns a woman, does anybody ever really want the facts?

Nightmare Alley [1947]

STANTON CARLISLE: You've got a heart as big as …

ZEENA KRUMBEIN: As big as an artichoke. A leaf for everyone.

Out of the Past [1947]

JACK FISHER: You know, a dame with a rod is like a guy with a knitting needle.

....

JEFF BAILEY/JEFF MARKHAM: You know, maybe I was wrong, and luck is like love: You have to go all the way to find it.

....

JEFF BAILEY/JEFF MARKHAM: You're like a leaf that the wind blows from one gutter to another.

....

ANN MILLER: She can't be all bad. No one is.

JEFF BAILEY/JEFF MARKHAM: Well, she comes the closest.

....

PETEY [WATCHES GIRL WALK AWAY]: Nice.

JEFF BAILEY/JEFF MARKHAM: Awfully cold around the heart.

....

MARNIE: Two things I can smell inside a hundred feet—burning hamburger and a romance.

....

JEFF BAILEY/JEFF MARKHAM: I didn't know you were so little.

KATHIE MOFFAT: I'm taller than Napoleon.

JEFF BAILEY/JEFF MARKHAM: You're prettier, too.

....

JEFF BAILEY/JEFF MARKHAM: You say to yourself, "How hot can it get?" Then, in Acapulco, you find out.

JEFF BAILEY/JEFF MARKHAM: How big a chump can you get to be? I was finding out.

JEFF BAILEY/JEFF MARKHAM: If I don't talk, I think. It's too late in life for me to start thinking.

JEFF BAILEY/JEFF MARKHAM: It was the bottom of the barrel, and I scraped it. But I didn't care. I had her.

JEFF BAILEY/JEFF MARKHAM: I never saw her in the daytime. We seemed to live by night. What was left of the day went away like a pack of cigarettes you smoked. I didn't know where she lived. I never followed her. All I ever had to go on was a place and time to see her again. I don't know what we were waiting for. Maybe we thought the world would end. Maybe we thought it was a dream and we'd wake up with a hangover in Niagara Falls.

KATHIE MOFFAT: I didn't know what I was doing. I … I didn't know anything except how much I hated him. But I didn't take anything. I didn't, Jeff. Don't you believe me?

JEFF BAILEY/JEFF MARKHAM: Baby, I don't care.

Quai des Orfèvres [1947]

aka *Jenny Lamour*

MARGUERITE CHAUFFORNIER MARTINEAU/JENNY LAMOUR [SINGS]: It drives them crazy with lust./In itself it wasn't astounding./It was simply a matter of thrust.

MARGUERITE CHAUFFORNIER MARTINEAU/JENNY LAMOUR: I'll take him for a ride. And what a ride.

MARGUERITE CHAUFFORNIER MARTINEAU/JENNY LAMOUR: Childhood friends, right. It starts with marbles and ends in the sack.

Railroaded! [1947]

JACKLAND AINSWORTH: Women should be struck regularly, like gongs. That's from Oscar Wilde, Clara.

CLARA: Give it back to him.

....

JACKLAND AINSWORTH: Listen to this: "You are not permitted to kill a woman who has injured you. But nothing forbids you to reflect that she is growing older every minute. You are avenged fourteen hundred and forty times a day." That's pretty good, eh, Clara?

CLARA: Pick the book you love best, ducky, and I'll see it's put in your coffin.

Ride the Pink Horse [1947]

LUCKY GAGIN: "Babies" is what you call dames. You understand that?

PILA: No.

LUCKY GAGIN: You understand what a human being is?

PILA: Yes.

LUCKY GAGIN: Well, they're not human beings. They're dead fish with a lot of perfume on them. You touch them and you always get stung. You always lose.

Singapore [1947]

LINDA GRAHAME/ANN VAN LEYDEN: So let me ruin you fast.

When it comes to women, we'll never have a chance.

—INSP. ANTOINE

Quai des Orfèvres

1947

MATT GORDON: How many have you ruined?

LINDA GRAHAME/ANN VAN LEYDEN: You're my last victim, darling.

They Won't Believe Me [1947]

LARRY BALLANTINE: She looked like a very special kind of dynamite, neatly wrapped in nylon and silk. Only I wasn't having any. I'd been too close to an explosion already. I was powder-shy.

The Two Mrs. Carrolls [1947]

SALLY MORTON CARROLL: Women are never wrong about women.

....

GEOFFREY CARROLL: You know, I have the strangest feeling this is the beginning of a beautiful hatred.

Call Northside 777 [1948]

P. J. McNEAL: You look nice. Will you marry me?

LAURA McNEAL: I did.

Force of Evil [1948]

JOE MORSE: If you need a broken man to love, break your husband.

Pitfall [1948]

JOHN FORBES: You were voted the prettiest girl in the class. I was voted the boy most likely to succeed. Something should happen to people like that.

....

SUE FORBES: You are the strangest husband I ever married.

....

MONA STEVENS: Terry, what do men like when they're sick?

TERRY: Lots of soup, plenty of babying, and some like bourbon.

White Heat [1948]

VERNA JARRETT: I'd look good in a mink coat, honey.

CODY JARRETT: You'd look good in a shower curtain.

Behind Locked Doors [1948]

KATHY LAWRENCE: I'm not so sure you're not really insane, with that kissing fixation of yours.

ROSS STEWART: Have you got a better way to go crazy?

The Bribe [1949]

RIGBY: Look, why don't you stop acting like you're alone in the jungle?

ELIZABETH HINTTEN: I'm not?

RIGBY: OK, so you are, but you'd be surprised how nice the birds and the beasts can be if you'll only give them a chance.

ELIZABETH HINTTEN: Tell me, Rigby, do you fly, walk on all fours . . . or crawl?

Criss Cross [1949]

STEVE THOMPSON: She's all right, she's just young.

MRS. THOMPSON: Huh. Some ways, she knows more than Einstein.

Deadly is the Female [1949] aka *Gun Crazy*

BART TARE: We go together, Laurie. I don't know why. Maybe like guns and ammunition go together.

PACKETT: Honey, I'll make money like you want me to. Big money. But it takes time, you gotta give me time.

ANNIE LAURIE STARR: You'll never make big money. You're a two-bit guy.

PACKETT: Honey, listen . . .

Will I never learn? The most dangerous thing about unmoral women is their tremendous, unused, and unpredictable reserve of honest feeling.

—ARTHUR "FRED" MARTINGALE

Rope of Sand 1949

ANNIE LAURIE STARR: No guts, nothing. I want action.

BLUEY-BLUEY [PUTS ON CLOWN MAKEUP]: It's just that some guys are born smart about women and some guys are born dumb.

BART TARE: Some guys are born clowns.

BLUEY-BLUEY: You were born dumb.

Rope of Sand [1949]

MIKE DAVIS: I went to bed with a seventy-five millimeter for three years, but now I sleep alone.

SUZANNE RENAUD/ANISENELETETTE DURINGEAUD: Now do you want to kiss me?

ARTHUR "FRED" MARTINGALE: Mmmm … no, I think not. You'd better keep your kisses for emergencies.

ARTHUR "FRED" MARTINGALE: How do I know I can trust you? I can't compete with love.

SUZANNE RENAUD/ANISENELETETTE DURINGEAUD: Diamonds are your business. But men are mine.

MIKE DAVIS: Come on, Red Riding Hood. Time to leave grandma.

MIKE DAVIS: If you ever tried to get away from me, I'd follow you 'til I wore the earth smooth.

Too Late for Tears [1949]

DANNY FULLER: Don't ever change, Tiger. I don't think I'd like you with a heart.

Armored Car Robbery [1950]

DET. DANNY RYAN: Imagine a dish like this married to a mug like Benny McBride. The naked and the dead.

Dark City [1950]

FRAN GARLAND: Why didn't you answer the phone?

DANNY HALEY: Nobody I wanted to talk to.

....

FRAN GARLAND: We're a great pair. I have no voice and you have no ear.

....

ARTHUR WINANT: She your girl?

DANNY HALEY: It's a free world. We go out.

In a Lonely Place [1950]

DIXON STEELE: I was born when she kissed me. I died when she left me. I lived a few weeks while she loved me.

....

FRANCES RANDOLPH: Remember how I used to read to you?

DIXON STEELE: Uh huh. Since then, I've learned to read by myself.

Kiss Tomorrow Goodbye [1950]

RALPH COTTER: And darling, by this time tomorrow, the words "small time" will have walked right out of your vocabulary. If we're still alive.

....

RALPH COTTER: Why, I thought you were the law-abiding type.

HOLIDAY CARLETON: I guess I'm just whatever you make me.

....

HOLIDAY CARLETON: You only said one true thing in your life, and that's when you said you were going away tonight. And you are. Many miles out of town and six feet under. All alone, with nobody to lie to. And you can kiss tomorrow goodbye.

....

RALPH COTTER: Hmm. Next time I come out with you, I'm gonna bring along an extra set of nerves.

Lonely Heart Bandits [1950]

BELLE: Just who would you expect to be introduced to for ten bucks? The Queen of Sheba?

ANGRY LUG: No, but I didn't expect to meet the Three Fates.

Sunset Boulevard [1950]

MAX VON MAYERLING: She was the greatest of them all. You wouldn't know, you're too young. In one week she received seventeen thousand fan letters. Men bribed her hairdresser to get a lock of her hair. There was a maharajah who came all the way from India to beg one of her silk stockings. Later he strangled himself with it.

1951–1960

Appointment With Danger [1951]

DODIE: You can put strings on good women or bad women. Can't do anything about the lazy ones.

AL GODDARD: You can beat 'em.

DODIE: They stay about the same.

Cry Danger [1951]

DELONG: I'm very disappointed in Darlene. She turned out to be a part-time model and a full-time pickpocket.

I said I liked it. I didn't say I wanted to kiss it.

—LAUREL GRAY

In a Lonely Place 1950

I still think
it would be wonderful
to have a man
love you so much
he'd kill for you.

—BARBARA MORTON

Strangers on a Train 1951

The Mob [1951]

DET. JOHNNY DAMICO: Mary, a successful marriage is based on a wife letting her husband lie a little. Now let's not get started on the wrong foot.

Angel Face [1952]

FRANK JESSUP: You know something: you're a pretty nice guy, for a girl.

Another Man's Poison [1952]

JANET FROBISHER: You have an unfair advantage. You know the way my brain works.

DR. HENDERSON: The dark recesses of the female mind? Huh. I can hardly claim to have penetrated that far.

Clash by Night [1952]

JERRY D'AMATO: Get something for that headache.

MAE DOYLE D'AMATO: Yeah, a new head.

....

MAE DOYLE D'AMATO: What do you want, Joe, my life's history? Here it is in four words: Big ideas, small results.

Don't Bother to Knock [1952]

JED TOWERS: You and your wife fight, argue all the time?

JOE THE BARTENDER: Some of the time she sleeps.

Kansas City Confidential [1952]

TIM FOSTER: No dames, understand?

TONY ROMANO: Look, friend, if you don't like it ... don't knock it.

JOE ROLFE: You're a nice girl but in case you're thinking or mothering me, forget it. I'm no stray dog you can pick up and I like my neck without a collar.

The Narrow Margin [1952]

DET. SGT. GUS FORBES: What kind of a dish?

DET. SGT. WALTER BROWN: Sixty-cent special. Cheap. Flashy. Strictly poison under the gravy.

DET. SGT. WALTER BROWN: Sister, I've known some pretty hard cases in my time; you make 'em all look like putty. You're not talking about a sack of gumdrops that's gonna be smashed—you're talking about a dame's life. You may think it's a funny idea for a woman with a kid to stop a bullet for you, only I'm not laughing.

MRS. NEALL: Where do you get off being so superior? Why shouldn't I take advantage of her—I want to live. If you had to step on someone to get something you wanted real bad, would you think twice about it?

DET. SGT. WALTER BROWN: Shut up.

MRS. NEALL: In a pig's eye you would. You're no different from me.

DET. SGT. WALTER BROWN: Shut up.

MRS. NEALL: Not 'til I tell you something, you cheap badge-pusher. When we started on this safari, you made it plenty clear I was just a job, and no joy in it, remember?

DET. SGT. WALTER BROWN: Yeah, and it still goes, double.

MRS. NEALL: Okay, keep it that way. I don't care whether you dreamed up this gag or not; you're going right along with it, so don't go soft on me. And once you handed out a line about poor Forbes getting killed, 'cause it was his duty. Well, it's your duty too. Even if this dame gets murdered.

DET. SGT. WALTER BROWN: You make me sick to my stomach.

MRS. NEALL: Well, use your own sink. And let me know when the target practice starts.

The Big Heat [1953]

KATIE BANNION [TALKS ABOUT DAUGHTER]: She's angelic all day but at night she's a holy terror.

DET. SGT. DAVE BANNION: That's the way I usually describe you.

....

VINCE STONE: Hey, that's a nice perfume.

DEBBY MARSH: Something new. Attracts mosquitoes and repels men.

....

DEBBY MARSH [EYES SEEDY HOTEL ROOM]: Hey, I like this. Early nothing.

....

DEBBY MARSH: You're about as romantic as a pair of handcuffs.

....

DEBBY MARSH: A scar isn't so bad. Not if it's only on one side. I can always go through life sideways.

....

DEBBY MARSH: We're sisters under the mink.

The Blue Gardenia [1953]

CRYSTAL CARPENTER: Honey, if a girl killed every man who got fresh with her, how much of the male population do you think there'd be left?

....

CRYSTAL CARPENTER: My phone number is GRanite 1466.

CASEY MAYO: I'll check with my numerologist before I call.

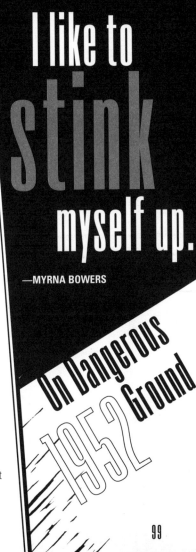

I like to **stink** myself up.

—MYRNA BOWERS

On Dangerous Ground 1952

SALLY ELLIS: Every girl ought to have birthdays—up to a certain point.

CRYSTAL CARPENTER: Now me, I've got my life with Homer. Drive-in dinner. Drive-in movie. And afterwards we go for a drive.

NORA LARKIN: You know, you don't appreciate Homer. I don't know exactly what they are, but he has a lot of good qualities.

HARRY PREBBLE [PLIES NORA WITH ALCOHOL]**:** These aren't really drinks. They're trade winds across cool lagoons. They're the Southern Cross above coral reefs. They're a lovely maiden bathing at the foot of a waterfall.

City That Never Sleeps [1953]

PENROD BIDDEL: I tried my best to help you the same as I helped others in the past. Ah, you. Lydia, when I first saw you …

LYDIA BIDDEL: I was selling coffee and hamburgers behind a counter in a railroad station.

PENROD BIDDEL: Yes, I had an hour to kill …

LYDIA BIDDEL: And you used it to murder years of my life.

The Glass Web [1953]

DON NEWELL: Sure, I liked that barbed-wire dress, one she said protected the property but didn't hide the view.

PAULA RAINER/PAULA ABBOTT: Look, Don, I've got nothing against married men. All of my best friends are married.

FRED ABBOTT: What man were you expecting? This is your husband, Mrs. Abbott.

PAULA RAINER/PAULA ABBOTT: I thought the farm inspectors took care of things like you at the state line.

Niagara [1953]

CUSTOMS OFFICER: How long do you plan to be here?

RAY CUTLER: Three days.

CUSTOMS OFFICER: Honeymooners?

POLLY CUTLER: That's right.

CUSTOMS OFFICER: That isn't liquor you have in that case under your coat, is it?

RAY CUTLER: Uh, books. I'm going to catch up on my reading.

CUSTOMS OFFICER: Reading.

Pickup on South Street [1953]

SKIP McCOY [KISSES CANDY]**:** Sometimes you look for oil, you hit a gusher.

Black Widow [1954]

NANNY ORDWAY: It's just that my mother always told me that if a girl could be at a party for thirty minutes without getting a man to talk to her, she might just as well go home and shoot herself. I've already been here twenty-five.

The Good Die Young [1954]

DORIS: Are you married?

EDDIE: Probably. Why?

DORIS: Oh, I just like to know what the weather's like before I put to sea.

Suddenly [1954]

POP BENSON: Ellen, will you please stop being a woman.

Kiss me, Mike.
I want you to kiss me.

Kiss me.

The liar's kiss that says I love you,
and means
something else.

—LILY CARVER

Kiss Me Deadly 1955

The Big Combo [1955]

POLICE LT. LEONARD DIAMOND: I treated her like a pair of gloves. I was cold, I called her up.

....

RITA: A woman doesn't care how a guy makes his living, only how he makes love.

The Big Knife [1955]

SMILEY COY: What do you think of women, kiddie?

CHARLES CASTLE: There's room in the world for 'em.

Les Diaboliques [1955] aka *Diabolique*

MR. RAYMOND: Tomorrow, Mademoiselle, I'll be all naked. And you ... how did you plan this long weekend?

....

MICHEL DELASALLE: Her. If you believe her. Two words, three lies.

Kiss Me Deadly [1955] aka *Mickey Spillane's Kiss Me Deadly*

MIKE HAMMER: You're never around when I need you.

VELDA: You never need me when I'm around.

The Night of the Hunter [1955]

ICEY SPOON [SPEWS ABOUT SEX]: When you've been married to a man forty years you know all that don't amount to a hill of beans. I've been married to my Walt that long and I swear in all that time I just lie there thinking about my canning.

....

ICEY SPOON: A woman's a fool to marry for that. That's somethin' for a man. The Good Lord never meant for a decent woman to want that. Not really want it. It's all just a fake and a pipe dream.

REV. HARRY POWELL: But there are things you do hate, Lord. Perfume-smellin' things, lacy things, things with curly hair.

The Phenix City Story [1955]

SID: What's he got I haven't?

ELLY: I don't know. I never went to kindergarten with you.

The Killing [1956]

GEORGE PEATTY: Been kinda sick today. I keep getting pains in my stomach.

SHERRY PEATTY: Maybe you got a hole in it, George. Do you suppose you have?

GEORGE PEATTY: A hole in it? How would I get a hole in my stomach?

SHERRY PEATTY: How would you get one in your head? Fix me a drink, George. I think I'm developing some pains myself.

GEORGE PEATTY: Tell me something, will you, Sherry? Tell me one thing. Why did you ever marry me anyway?

SHERRY PEATTY: Oh, George, when a man has to ask his wife that, well, he just hasn't met her yet. That's all. Why talk about it? Maybe it's all to the good in the long turn. After all, if people didn't have headaches, what would happen to the aspirin industry?

SHERRY PEATTY: You don't understand me, Johnny. You don't know me very well.

JOHNNY CLAY: I know you like a book. You're a no-good nosey little tramp. You'd sell out your own mother for a piece of fudge.

Sweet Smell of Success [1957]

RITA: What am I, a bowl of fruit? A tangerine that peels in a minute?

SUSAN HUNSECKER: Who could love a man who makes you jump through burning hoops like a trained poodle?

J.J. HUNSECKER: Everyone knows Manny Davis except for Mrs. Manny Davis.

The Lineup [1958]

DOROTHY BRADSHAW: What kind of man are you?

JULIAN: See? You cry. That's why women have no place in society. Women are weak. Crime's aggressive and so is the law.

Lonelyhearts [1958]

JUSTY SARGENT: Has anybody ever tried to figure out how many tears you cry in a lifetime?

Vertigo [1958]

MIDGE WOOD: I'm going back to my first love, painting.

DET. JOHN "SCOTTIE" FERGUSON: Good for you. I always said you were wasting your time in the underwear department.

MIDGE WOOD: It's a living.

DET. JOHN "SCOTTIE" FERGUSON: What's this doohickey?

MIDGE WOOD: It's a brassiere. You know all about those things. You're a big boy now.

You're my wife but also the widow of our early romance. You wear your gay plumage hoping one day for the resurrection so that you may greet it with the freshness of a bride.

—WILLIAM SHRIKE

Lonelyhearts 1958

Anyone ever tell you . . .

—JOEL

Yeah, they told me.

—GLORIA

They Shoot Horses, Don't They?
1969

1961–1970

Blast of Silence [1961]

NIGHTCLUB SINGER [SINGS]: Met a girl/A year ago/She knew everything there was to know/Her eyes were grey, her hair was jet/Oh, my evil baby, I can't forget./So I'm dressed in black all the time/Dressed in black all the time.

Cape Fear [1962]

DIANE TAYLOR: Max Cady, what I like about you is, you're rock bottom. I wouldn't expect you to understand this, but it's a great comfort for a girl to know she could not possibly sink any lower.

....

DIANE TAYLOR: What would you know about scenery? Or beauty? Or any of the things that really make life worth living? You're just an animal. Coarse. Lustful. Barbaric.

MAX CADY: Keep right on talking, honey. I like it when you run me down like that.

Mélodie en Sous-Sol [1963]
aka *Any Number Can Win*

COUNTESS DOUBLIANOFF: I must be getting old. I can no longer tell a gentleman from a pimp.

....

CHARLES: I've given you problems more than once with my fits of jealousy. But,

It's a Bitter Little World

deep down I've always trusted you.

GINETTE: Trust like that must mean I'm getting on in years.

The Killers [1964]

SHEILA FARR: I like you. Do I have to write a book?

Lady in Cement [1968]

SHIPMATE: [TALKS ABOUT AN UNDERWATER DIVE]: You must have seen something down there.

TONY ROME: Yeah, a dead blonde.

SHIPMATE: A dead blonde? Was she pretty?

TONY ROME: She's one blonde I know didn't have more fun.

....

PAUL MUNGAR: Go lose yourself.

MOLL: What am I supposed to do?

PAUL MUNGAR: Read a book.

MOLL: A whole hour?

PAUL MUNGAR: Look at the pictures.

1971–1980

Chinatown [1974]

EVELYN CROSS MULWRAY: I'll tell you … I'll tell you the truth.

JAKE GITTES: Good. What's her name?

EVELYN CROSS MULWRAY: Katherine.

JAKE GITTES: Katherine who?

EVELYN CROSS MULWRAY: She's my daughter.

JAKE GITTES [SLAPS HER]: I said I want the truth.

EVELYN CROSS MULWRAY: She's my sister.
[GITTES SLAPS HER]

EVELYN CROSS MULWRAY: She's my daughter.
[GITTES SLAPS HER AGAIN]

EVELYN CROSS MULWRAY: My sister. My daughter . . .

JAKE GITTES [SLAPS HER AGAIN]: I said I want the truth.

EVELYN CROSS MULWRAY: She's my sister and my daughter.

EVELYN CROSS MULWRAY: Father and I . . . understand? Or is it too tough for you?

Farewell, My Lovely [1975]

PHILIP MARLOWE: I figured there must have been about a couple of hundred thousand girls who were cute as lace pants who passed through Hollywood in the last seven years, and most of them had taken their pants off at one time or another while trying to make the grade.

....

PHILIP MARLOWE: I don't know. Ever since I saw that movie *King Kong,* I've been a sucker for any gorilla that falls in love with a girl.

Night Moves [1975]

ARLENE IVERSON: Are you the kind of detective who, once you get on a case, nothing can get you off it—bribes, beatings, the allure of a woman's body . . .

HARRY MOSEBY: That was during the old days, before we had the union.

....

PAULA ELLMAN [TALKS ABOUT SMUGGLING]: I got into it because I got involved with Tom. I got involved with Tom because he was the only man around who got nicer when he got drunk.

....

ELLEN MOSEBY: If you don't go now, you can't come back.

Her hair was the color of gold in old paintings. She had a full set of curves, which nobody had been able to improve on. She was giving me the kind of look I could feel in my hip pocket.

—PHILIP MARLOWE

Farewell, My Lovely 1975

What's wrong with tits?

—COSMO VITELLI

The Killing of a Chinese Bookie 1976

ARLENE IVERSON: You can join me. It's a big bath.

HARRY MOSEBY: Maybe some other time when I'm feeling really dirty.

HARRY MOSEBY: You got any idea where she could be? She visiting friends? She meditating? She join a commune?

QUENTIN: Delly's idea of a commune is her and the guy on top of her.

MARV ELLMAN: You're a really straight guy and I'm gonna tell ya, I want that kid the hell out of here. You see I uh, I got pretty foolish with her. You've seen her. God, there oughta be a law.

HARRY MOSEBY: There is.

The Killing of a Chinese Bookie [1976]

COSMO VITELLI: I'm a club owner. I deal in girls.

Taxi Driver [1976]

IRIS STEENSMA: When that cigarette burns out, your time is up.

TRAVIS BICKLE: I realize now how much she's just like the others. Cold and distant. Many people are like that. Women for sure. They're like a union.

Série Noire [1979]

FRANK POUPART: You're not just sizzling, you're the Towering Inferno.

1981–1990

Body Heat [1981]

MATTY WALKER: My temperature runs a couple of degrees high—around a hundred. I don't mind. The engine or something.

NED RACINE: Maybe you need a tune-up.

MATTY WALKER: Don't tell me—you have just the right tool.

....

MATTY WALKER: I'm a married woman.

NED RACINE: Meaning what?

MATTY WALKER: Meaning I'm not looking for company.

NED RACINE: Then you should have said "I'm a happily married woman."

....

MATTY WALKER: You're not too smart, are you? I like that in a man.

....

NED RACINE: What else do you like? Lazy? Ugly? Horny? I got 'em all.

....

NED RACINE: You look good in black.

Coup de Torchon [1981] aka *Clean Slate*

LUCIEN CORDIER: You'll manage. I'm sure of that. You could make a mint just doing what you like best. Which, by the way, you do better than any woman I've known. And being as we'll probably never see each other again, I'll be glad to have a last quick one with you, even though you're a fugitive.

Cutter's Way [1981]

RICHARD BONE: I don't like you when you're stoned.

MAUREEN "MO" CUTTER: Hey, Rich, I don't like you when I'm straight.

MAUREEN "MO" CUTTER: Speaking of which, you're home awfully early, aren't you? Couldn't you find a matron with a taste for gutter squalor?

The Postman Always Rings Twice [1981]

CORA PAPADAKIS: He wants to have a baby ... How'm I gonna do that, Frank?

Thief [1981]

FRANK: You're marking time, is what you are. You're backing off. You're hiding out. You're waiting for a bus that you hope never comes because you don't want to get on it anyway, because you don't want to go anywhere, all right?

JESSIE: Do you have a license for this?

True Confessions [1981]

BRENDA: I need you like I need another fuck.

Blood Simple [1984]

ABBY: Marty said I always had too much personality. He was never big on personality.

The Grifters [1990]

MYRA LANGTRY: I'm Roy's friend.

LILLY DILLON: I imagine you're lots of people's friend.

MYRA LANGTRY: Oh, oh, of course. Now that I see you in the light you're plenty old enough to be Roy's mother.

LILLY DILLON: Aren't we all?

....

ROY DILLON: I have seen women like you before, baby. You double-talk and you are sharp as a razor and you get what you want or else. But you don't make it work forever. Sooner or later the lightning hits and I'm not going to be around when it hits you.

Nobody **fucks** with me.

—FRANK BOOTH

Well, maybe if you find the **right girl**.

—JEFFREY BEAUMONT

Blue Velvet
1986

Miller's Crossing [1990]

VERNA: Leo's got the right idea. I like him. He's honest and he's got a heart.

TOM REAGAN: Then it's true what they say: opposites attract.

....

VERNA: I like you, Tom. I never met anybody made being a son of a bitch such a point of pride.

The Two Jakes [1990]

JAKE GITTES: But stay in this business long enough and every street leads to a place you'd like to forget. Every case brings back memories of what you should have done and what might have been. And every skirt reminds you of another woman. Or, if you've got it bad enough, the same woman.

....

JAKE GITTES: Hell, everybody makes mistakes. But if you marry one, they expect you to pay for it the rest of your life.

....

JAKE GITTES: Get down on your knees. Get your ass up in the air and don't move until I tell you.

1991–2000

Dead Again [1991]

MIKE CHURCH: Why does she want to kill me now?

COZY CARLISLE: Why do women do anything?

Romeo Is Bleeding [1993]

JACK GRIMALDI: Like I used to say, whoever you shoot, you may as well marry them. 'Cause you're tied to them for life 'til the end of their life or the end of yours.

SHERI: Jack, you know what the best part of making it with a cop is? You got two guns. One for me and one for them.

JACK GRIMALDI: Can I tell you what makes love so frightening? It's that you don't own it—it owns you.

True Romance [1993]

CLARENCE WORLEY: You're a whore ?

ALABAMA WHITMAN/WORLEY: No, I'm a call-girl. And there's a difference, you know.

CLARENCE WORLEY: Man, I can't tell you how relieved I was when you took off your dress, you … you didn't have a dick.

ALABAMA WHITMAN/WORLEY: Amid the chaos of that day, when all I could hear was the thunder of gunshots, and all I could smell was the violence in the air, I look back and am amazed that my thoughts were so clear and true, that three words went through my mind endlessly, repeating themselves like a broken record: you're so cool, you're so cool, you're so cool. And sometimes Clarence asks me what I would have done if he had died, if that bullet had been two inches more to the left. To this, I always smile, as if I'm not going to satisfy him with a response. But I always do. I tell him of how I would want to die, but that the anguish and the want of death would fade like the stars at dawn, and that things would be much as they are now. Perhaps. Except maybe I wouldn't have named our son Elvis.

The Last Seduction [1994]

BRIDGET GREGORY/WENDY KROY: Who's a girl gotta suck around here to get a drink?

BRIDGET GREGORY/WENDY KROY: Could you leave? Please?

MIKE SWALE: Well, I haven't finished charming you yet.

You still a lawyer,
Frank?

—BRIDGET GREGORY/WENDY KROY

Yeah.

You still a
self-serving bitch?

—FRANK GRIFFITH

The Last Seduction 1994

BRIDGET GREGORY/WENDY KROY: You haven't started.

....

MIKE SWALE: I'm hung like a horse. Think about it.

BRIDGET GREGORY/WENDY KROY: Let's see.

MIKE SWALE: Excuse me?

BRIDGET GREGORY/WENDY KROY: Mr. Ed, let's see.

MIKE SWALE: Look, I tried to be nice. I can see that's something you're not.

BRIDGET GREGORY/WENDY KROY: No, I'm trying. I can be very nice when I try. Sit down.

MIKE SWALE: OK, maybe we just got off to a bad start. I know Ray's put plenty of people in a …

[BRIDGET UNZIPS HIS FLY]

MIKE SWALE: What are you doing?

BRIDGET GREGORY/WENDY KROY: I believe what we're looking for is a certain horse-like quality?

....

BRIDGET GREGORY/WENDY KROY: You're my designated fuck.

MIKE SWALE: Designated fuck? They make cards for that? What if I want to be more than your designated fuck?

BRIDGET GREGORY/WENDY KROY: I'll designate someone else.

....

MIKE SWALE: I'm still trying to decide whether you're a total bitch or not.

BRIDGET GREGORY/WENDY KROY: I'm a total fucking bitch.

....

BRIDGET GREGORY/WENDY KROY: What are you saying?

FRANK GRIFFITH: My lips moving too fast for you?

BRIDGET GREGORY/WENDY KROY: Not fast enough, as I recall.

....

FRANK GRIFFITH: Anybody check you for a heartbeat lately?

Pulp Fiction [1994]

BUTCH COOLIDGE: Will you hand me a dry towel, Miss Beautiful Tulip?

FABIENNE: Ah, I like that. I like tulip. Tulip is much better than Mongoloid.

Shallow Grave [1994]

ALEX LAW: God, you two are sensitive. All I'm doing is implying some kind of ugly sordid sexual liaison. I'd be proud of that sort of thing.

Heat [1995]

JUSTINE HANNA: You don't live with me, you live among the remains of dead people. You sift through the detritus, you read the terrain, you search for signs of passing, for the scent of your prey … and then you hunt them down. That's the only thing you're committed to. The rest is the mess you leave as you pass through.

....

LT. VINCENT HANNA: 'Cause I gotta hold on to my angst. I preserve it because I need it. It keeps me sharp, on the edge, where I gotta be.

The Underneath [1995]

MICHAEL CHAMBERS: He treat you OK?

RACHEL: Not as well as guys without money.

Bound [1996]

SUE THE BARTENDER: Well, well. It's been a long time, Cork.

CORKY: Five years, two months, sixteen days. How ya doing, Sue?

SUE THE BARTENDER: Like shit. Well, now that we're all caught up, can I buy you a drink?

Fargo [1996]

HOOKER: Well, the little guy, he was kinda funny-lookin'.

POL. CHIEF MARGE GUNDERSON: In what way?

118

HOOKER: I dunno, just funny-lookin'.

POL. CHIEF MARGE GUNDERSON: Can ya be any more specific?

HOOKER: I couldn't really say. He wasn't circumcised.

POL. CHIEF MARGE GUNDERSON: Was he funny-lookin' apart from that?

L.A. Confidential [1997]

SGT. JACK VINCENNES: Oh, great. You get the girl, I get the coroner.

Lost Highway [1997]

PETE DAYTON: I want you.

RENEE MADISON/ALICE WAKEFIELD: You'll never have me.

The Spanish Prisoner [1997]

JOSEPH A. "JOE" ROSS: I ain't looking for an office romance. All I want is an umbrella in my drink.

U Turn [1997]

GRACE MCKENNA: Come on, baby, what can I do to make you feel more relaxed?

BOBBY COOPER: You can give me my gun back.

The Big Lebowski [1998]

THE DUDE: Jackie Treehorn treats objects like women, man.

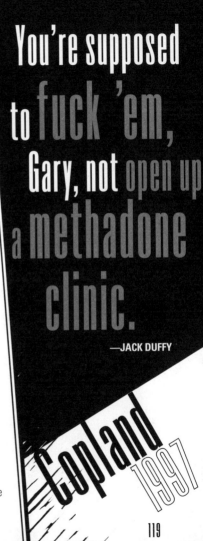

You're supposed to fuck 'em, Gary, not open up a methadone clinic.

—JACK DUFFY

Copland 1997

Sir, could I interest you in a battery-operated vagina?

—MAX CALIFORNIA

Well, it's tempting, but no thanks.

—TOM WELLES

OK, I hate to see you caught in one of those everyday situations that calls for a battery-operated vagina and you just don't have one. You know what I mean?

—MAX CALIFORNIA

I'll risk it.

—TOM WELLES

8MM 1997

JACKIE TREEHORN: New technology permits us to do very exciting things in interactive erotic software. Wave of the future, Dude. One hundred percent electronic.

THE DUDE: Hmm. Well, I still jerk off manually.

Clay Pigeons [1998]

AGT. SHELBY: You know what? No offense, but this seat is saved.

LESTER LONG: Who for?

AGT. SHELBY: First guy not wearing denim.

Following [1998]

BILL: Buy you a drink?

THE BLONDE: Yes, but you can't sleep with me.

Rounders [1998]

LESTER "WORM" MURPHY: She's really got him by the balls.

PETRA: That's not so bad, is it?

LESTER "WORM" MURPHY: It depends on the grip.

....

MIKE MCDERMOTT [HITS HIS GIRLFRIEND UP FOR SEX]: I'll be really quick. You won't feel a thing.

Best Laid Plans [1999]

BRYCE: Everybody sucks but us.

....

BRYCE: If she press charges, I will go to jail.

NICK: Well, I guess a second date's out of the question then.

The Limey [1999]

ADHARA: You're not specific enough to be a person.

STACY: Wonder what it's like to have tits.

2001–2005

Heist [2001]

JOE MOORE: She could talk her way out of a sunburn.

MICKEY BERGMAN: You mind if I say something personal? Your wife's a whore.

The Man Who Wasn't There [2001]

EDWARD "ED" CRANE: It was only a couple of weeks later she suggested we get married. I said, "Don't you want to get to know me more?" She said, "Why? Does it get better?"

The Quiet American [2002]

THOMAS FOWLER: I should have realized how saving a country and saving a woman would be the same thing to someone like Pyle.

ALDEN PYLE: I trusted you, Thomas.

THOMAS FOWLER: Always a mistake when there's a woman involved.

The Cooler [2003]

SHELLY KAPLOW: I can make you disappear like that. And not one fucking person would miss you. Not one fuckin' person.

I only wanted to get laid. Instead I'm getting fucked.

—BRYCE

Best Laid Plans 1999

She smells like **angels** ought to smell. —MARV

Sin City 2005

NATALIE BELISARIO: Bernie would.

NATALIE [LOOKS AT HER CUT-UP FACE IN THE REARVIEW MIRROR]: Oh my God.

BERNIE: Hey. You look in the mirror, you don't like what you see, don't believe it. Look in my eyes, I am the only mirror you're ever gonna need. You look in my eyes, Natalie.

Sin City [2005]

JOHN HARTIGAN: An old man dies. A young woman lives. A fair trade. I love you, Nancy.

PRIEST: While you're at it, ask yourself if that corpse of a slut is worth dying for.

MARV [SHOOTS PRIEST]: Worth dying for. [SHOOTS PRIEST AGAIN] Worth killing for. [SHOOTS PRIEST ONE MORE TIME] Worth going to hell for. Amen.

MARV: When I find out who did it, it won't be quick and quiet like it was with you. It'll be loud and nasty: My kind of kill. And when his eyes go dead, the hell I send him to will seem like heaven after what I've done to him. I love you, Goldie.

DWIGHT: The fire, baby. It'll burn us both. There's no place in this world for our kind of fire. My warrior woman. My Valkyrie. You'll always be mine. Always and never.

I have the perfect weapon right here:

These two hands.

—BRUNO ANTHONY

Strangers on a Train 1951

CHAPTER THREE

The Brutality and the Barbs

1941–1950

The Maltese Falcon [1941]

WILMER COOK: Keep on riding me. They're gonna be picking iron out of your liver.

SAM SPADE: The cheaper the crook, the gaudier the patter, eh?

JOEL CAIRO: You ... you bungled it. You and your stupid attempt to buy it. Kemedov found out how valuable it was. No wonder we had such an easy time stealing it. You ... you imbecile. You bloated idiot. You stupid fathead you ...

When you're **slapped**, you'll **take it** and **like it.**

—SAM SPADE

The Maltese 1941 Falcon

The Glass Key [1942]

CLYDE MATTHEWS: Isn't all this beating likely to be fatal?

NICK VARNA: Not unless we want it to be.

Shadow of a Doubt [1943]

JOSEPH NEWTON: We're not talking about killing people. Herb's talking about killing me and I'm talking about killing him.

Double Indemnity [1944]

WALTER NEFF: I never knew that murder could smell like honeysuckle.

....

BARTON KEYES: I picked you for the job, not because I think you're so darned smart, but because I thought you were a shade less dumb than the rest of the outfit. Guess I was wrong. You're not smarter, Walter … you're just a little taller.

....

WALTER NEFF: Suddenly it came over me that everything would go wrong. It sounds crazy, Keyes, but it's true, so help me. I couldn't hear my own footsteps. It was the walk of a dead man.

....

BARTON KEYES: They've committed a murder and it's not like taking a trolley ride together where they can get off at different stops. They're stuck with each other and they've got to ride all the way to the end of the line and it's a one-way trip and the last stop is the cemetery.

Laura [1944]

WALDO LYDECKER: I should be sincerely sorry to see my neighbor's children devoured by wolves.

....

WALDO LYDECKER: I cannot stand these morons any longer.

Murder, My Sweet [1944]

PHILIP MARLOWE: I caught the blackjack right behind my ear. A black pool opened up at my feet. I dived in. It had no bottom.

....

PHILIP MARLOWE: I felt pretty good—like an amputated leg.

....

HELEN GRAYLE/VELMA: You know, this'll be the first time I've ever killed anyone I knew so little and liked so well.

Phantom Lady [1944]

JACK MARLOW: What a place. I can feel the rats in the walls.

The Big Sleep [1946]

PHILIP MARLOWE: My, my, my. Such a lot of guns around town and so few brains.

....

GENERAL STERNWOOD: You knew him too?

PHILIP MARLOWE: Yes, in the old days, when he used to run rum out of Mexico and I was on the other side. We used to swap shots between drinks, or drinks between shots, whichever you like.

....

PHILIP MARLOWE: You know what he'll do when he finds out, don't you? He'll beat my teeth out, then kick me in the stomach for mumbling.

The Stranger [1946]

PROF. CHARLES RANKIN/FRANZ KINDLER: Murder can be a chain, Mary, one link leading to another until it circles your neck. Red was digging at the grave of the man I killed. Yes, your little man.

MARY LONGSTREET: You killed him?

PROF. CHARLES RANKIN/FRANZ KINDLER: With these hands. The same hands that have held you close to me.

....

MR. POTTER: 'Course, he's changed some. Being buried in the earth does it.

Kiss of Death [1947]

TOMMY UDO: You know what I do to squealers? I let 'em have it in the belly, so they can roll around for a long time thinkin' it over. You're worse than him, tellin' me he's comin' back. Ya lyin' old hag.

Lady in the Lake [1947]

LT. DEGARMOT: You stick your nose into my business and you'll wake up in an alley with the cats looking at you.

....

ADRIENNE FROMSETT: You look like an emergency.

PHILIP MARLOWE: Well, It's an old sickness. Reoccurring black eyes.

....

PHILIP MARLOWE: At least he had the decency to hit me above the Mason and Dixon line.

Out of the Past [1947]

JIMMY: I was going to kill you.

JEFF BAILEY/JEFF MARKHAM: Who isn't?

Railroaded! [1947]

JACKLAND AINSWORTH: You can't settle everything with a gun, you know. Some people you gotta get along with.

You can't just go round **killing people** whenever the mood strikes you. —MARTY WATERMAN
It's not feasible.

Born to Kill 1947

Force of Evil [1948]

LEO MORSE: All that Cain did to Abel was kill him.

The Naked City [1948]

DET. LT. DAN MULDOON: You're getting quite a slapping around these days, aren't you?

Raw Deal [1948]

RICK COYLE: When a man screams, I don't like it, especially a friend. He might scream loud enough for the D.A. to hear. I don't want to hurt the D.A.'s ears. He's sensitive.

Abandoned [1949]

LITTLE GUY DECOLA: There's a rumor going around town that I'm getting soft. Whenever that happens, I always cut a couple of throats just to prove a point.

Deadly Is the Female [1949] aka *Gun Crazy*

ANNIE LAURIE STARR: You shouldn't have shot him up 'til Wednesday.
BART TARE: Why Wednesday?
ANNIE LAURIE STARR: Payday.

Follow Me Quietly [1949]

POLICE SGT. ART COLLINS: I once knew a man used to cut off cats' tails. He didn't like cats. … The Judge cuts off people's wind. He don't like people, I guess.

The Set-Up [1949]

STOKER: Yeah, top spot. And I'm just one punch away.

JULIE: I remember the first time you told me that. You were just one punch away from the title shot then. Don't you see, Bill, you'll always be just one punch away.

Too Late for Tears [1949]

JANE PALMER: What do I call you, besides "stupid"?

DANNY FULLER: "Stupid" will do if you don't bruise easily.

White Heat [1949]

ROY PARKER: You wouldn't kill me in cold blood, would ya?

CODY JARRETT: No, I'll let ya warm up a little.

....

CODY JARRETT: If that battery's dead, it will have company.

....

CODY JARRETT: You know something, Verna, if I turn my back for long enough for Big Ed to put a hole in it, there'd be a hole in it.

The Asphalt Jungle [1950]

DR. SWANSON: He hasn't got enough blood left in him to keep a chicken alive.

D.O.A. [1950]

FRANK BIGELOW: I want to report a murder.

HOMICIDE CAPT.: Sit down. Where was this murder committed?

FRANK BIGELOW: San Francisco, last night.

HOMICIDE CAPT.: Who was murdered?

FRANK BIGELOW: I was.

Sunset Boulevard [1950]

JOE GILLIS: Funny, how gentle people get with you once you're dead.

In Italy for 30 years under the Borgias they had warfare, terror, murder, and bloodshed, but they produced Michelangelo, Leonardo da Vinci, and the Renaissance. In Switzerland they had brotherly love—they had 500 years of democracy and peace, and what did that produce? The cuckoo clock. —HARRY LIME

The Third Man 1949

Where the Sidewalk Ends [1950]

MORGAN TAYLOR/MORGAN PAINE: I'll fix your head. Come with me.

DET. SGT. MARK DIXON: I suggest you use an axe.

1951–1960

Cry Danger [1951]

LOUIE CASTRO: Would you kill me, Rocky?

ROCKY MULLOY: Wouldn't you?

Strangers on a Train [1951]

GUY HAINES: I may be old-fashioned, but I thought murder was against the law.

BRUNO ANTHONY: Don't worry, I'm not going to shoot you, Mr. Haines. It might disturb Mother.

....

BRUNO ANTHONY: You don't mind if I borrow your neck for moment do you?

The Big Heat [1953]

TIERNEY: They come and go like flies.

DET. SGT. DAVE BANNION: Only this fly got herself strangled.

TIERNEY: These things happen, Sergeant.

Suddenly [1954]

JOHNNY BARON: Sheriff, if you think I have any qualms about killing this kid, you couldn't be more wrong. The thing about killing him, or you, or her, or him is that I wouldn't be getting paid for it—and I don't like giving anything away for free.

JOHNNY BARON: When you've got a gun you are a sort of god. If you had the gun I'd be the chump and you'd be the god.

Bad Day at Black Rock [1955]

RENO SMITH: Tim, you've got the body of a hippo but the brain of a rabbit. Now don't overtax it.

The Big Combo [1955]

MINGO: Shoots me with my own gun, that's what gets me.

The Night of the Hunter [1955]

REV. HARRY POWELL [TALKS TO GOD]: Not that you mind the killings. Your book is full of killings.

The Harder They Fall [1956]

BUDDY BRANNEN: When I butcher a guy, I want the whole world to know it.

Please Murder Me [1956]

SGT. HILL: How come everybody always shoots everybody else in self-defense?

Sweet Smell of Success [1957]

SIDNEY FALCO: You're blind, Mr. Magoo.

STEVE DALLAS: Mr. Hunsecker, you've got more twists than a barrel of pretzels.

Lonelyhearts [1958]

WILLIAM SHRIKE: You're as important to this department as my tonsils—which I lost some forty years ago.

WILLIAM SHRIKE: He'll steal my fillings when I lie dead on in the street.

FLORENCE SHRIKE: Then why keep him?

WILLIAM SHRIKE: Because I enjoy seeing youth betray their promises. It lights up all the numbers on my pinball machine. Any other questions?

1961–1970

The Manchurian Candidate [1962]

DR. YEN LO: His brain has not only been washed, as they say, it has been dry-cleaned.

Mélodie en Sous-Sol [1963]

aka *Any Number Can Win*

CHARLES: In a tense situation, if you speak firmly with a gun in your fist, nobody will answer back. Statistics bear me out.

The Killers [1964]

CHARLIE STROM: There's only one guy who's not afraid to die. That's a guy who's already dead.

In Cold Blood [1967]

PERRY SMITH: I thought Mr. Clutter was a very nice man … I thought so right up to the moment I cut his throat.

Do me a favor, will you? Keep away from the **windows**. Somebody might … blow you a **kiss.**

—VELDA

Kiss Me Deadly 1955

Lady in Cement [1968]

WALDO GRONSKY [THROTTLES TINY TONY ROME]: You got anything else funny to say?

TONY ROME: Yeah, what sells best, the frozen peas or the corn? Ho-ho-ho.

They Shoot Horses, Don't They? [1969]

FIRST COP: Why'd you do it, kid?

ROBERT: Because she asked me to.

SECOND COP: Obliging bastard. That the only reason you got, kid?

ROBERT: They shoot horses, don't they?

1971–1980

Badlands [1973]

HOLLY SARGIS: How is he?

KIT CARRUTHERS: I got him in the stomach.

HOLLY SARGIS: Is he upset?

KIT CARRUTHERS: He didn't say nothing to me about it.

Chinatown [1974]

JAKE GITTES: Mulvihill. What are you doing here?

CLAUDE MULVIHILL: They shut my water off. What's it to you?

JAKE GITTES: How'd you find out about it? You don't drink it. You don't take a bath in it. They wrote you a letter. But then you have to be able to read.

My people don't **crucify** anybody.

Crucifying is **wop** shit.

—DOC JOHNSON

Across 110th Street 1972

Each night when I return
the cab to the garage
I have to clean the cum
off the back seat.
Some nights I clean up the
blood.

—TRAVIS BICKLE

Taxi Driver 1976

DET. LOACH: What happened to your nose, Gittes? Somebody slam a bedroom window on it?

JAKE GITTES: Nope. Your wife got excited. She crossed her legs a little too quick. You understand what I mean, pal?

JAKE GITTES: You're dumber than you think I think you are.

The Conversation [1974]

HARRY CAUL: I'm not afraid of death, but I am afraid of murder.

Farewell, My Lovely [1975]

PHILIP MARLOWE [INTERROGATES MADAM]: What's the matter? Cathouse got your tongue?

PHILIP MARLOWE: OK, Marlowe, I said, you're a tough guy. Six feet of iron man. One hundred and ninety pounds stripped and with your face washed. Hard muscles and no glass jaw. You can take it. You've been sapped down twice, you've been shot full of hop and kept under it until you were as crazy as two waltzing mice. And what does that amount to? Routine. Now let's see you do something really tough, like getting up.

Taxi Driver [1976]

TAXI PASSENGER: Did you ever see what a forty-four Magnum pistol can do to a woman's face?

TRAVIS BICKLE: All the animals come out at night. Whores, skunk pussies, buggers, queens, fairies, dopers, junkies. Sick, venal. Someday a real rain will come and wash all the scum off the streets.

The Long Good Friday [1980]

HAROLD: You don't crucify people. Not on Good Friday.

1981–1990

True Confessions [1981]

DET. FRANK CROTTY [LOOKS AT CORPSE CHOPPED IN TWO]: I think the butler did it.

....

DET. TOM SPELLACY: Get me a list of sex crimes with the same MO.

RADIO DISPATCHER: That'll take a while, Sergeant.

DET. TOM SPELLACY: What do you mean, it'll take a while? She was cut in two. You think it's an epidemic, like flu?

....

DET. FRANK CROTTY: Nothing like a stiff for making me crave Chinese food.

Body Heat [1981]

PETER LOWENSTEIN: You started using your incompetence as a weapon.

Coup de Torchon [1981]

aka *Clean Slate*

LUCIEN CORDIER: What are you hunting?

LEONELLI: Nothing, jerk. We're shooting stiffs.

LE PERON: Doesn't bother them, and it's fun for us. When dysentery's cured, we'll find a new sport.

....

LUCIEN CORDIER [KICKS MAN HE JUST SHOT]: I know kicking a dying man isn't very nice. But first, I wanted to. And second, there's no risk involved.

....

ROSE: But that's horrible.

LUCIEN CORDIER: At first, you're right, it is horrible, but then you start to think about a thousand other different things: Starving kids, girls sold as slaves for a mirror, women whose sex is sewn up … and you start thinking God created murder out of pure kindness.

She wouldn't talk to him.
—BOBBY SHY

How do you know that?
—ALAN RAIMY

Because she's a friend of mine.
And she knows if I found out,
I'd throw her dead ass
off a roof. —BOBBY SHY

52 Pick-Up 1986

Hey,
what's going on?
Can you
hear that?

—MR. BLONDE

Reservoir Dogs 1992

144

At Close Range [1986]

BRAD WHITEWOOD, JR.: Is this the gun you used on everybody? On me? Is this the family gun, Dad?

The Grifters [1990]

BOBO JUSTUS: Tell me about the oranges, Lilly, while you put those in the towel.

LILLY DILLON: You hit a person with the oranges wrapped in a towel. They get big, ugly-looking bruises. But they don't really get hurt, not if you do it right. It's for working scams against the insurance companies.

BOBO JUSTUS: And if you do it wrong?

LILLY DILLON: It can louse up your insides. You can get puh … puh … puh …

BOBO JUSTUS: What?

LILLY DILLON: … permanent damage.

BOBO JUSTUS: You never shit right again. Bring me the towel.

The Two Jakes [1990]

CAPT. LOU ESCOBAR: And then what happened?

JAKE GITTES: What usually happens when somebody pulls a gun, Lou. Everybody ducks.

....

LARRY WALSH: Does that mean he wants you to prove your own client is guilty of murder?

JAKE GITTES: Yeah.

LARRY WALSH: Well, is that ethical?

JAKE GITTES: Larry, he's a lawyer.

....

JAKE GITTES: Besides, I wouldn't extort a nickel from my worst enemy. That's where I draw the line.

DET. LOACH: Well, I'll tell you, Jake. I knew a whore once. For the right amount of money, she'd piss in a guy's face. But she wouldn't shit on his chest. You see, that's where she drew the line.

JAKE GITTES: Well, Junior, all I can say is: I hope she wasn't too much of a disappointment to you.

1991–2000

Dead Again [1991]

COZY CARLISLE: I mean, karmically, self-defense is quite cool.

Red Rock West [1992]

SUZANNE BROWN/ANN McCORD: Marriage is just a state of mind.

MICHAEL WILLIAMS: Not in Texas.

Reservoir Dogs [1992]

MR. BLONDE: All you can do is pray for a quick death, which you ain't gonna to get.

....

MR. BLONDE: Are you gonna bark all day, little doggy, or are you gonna bite?

....

MR. BLONDE: If you're talking like a bitch, I'm gonna slap you like a bitch.

True Romance [1993]

VIRGIL: Now the first time you kill somebody, that's the hardest. I don't give a shit if you're fuckin' Wyatt Earp or Jack the Ripper. Remember that guy in Texas? The guy up in that fuckin' tower killed all them people? I'll bet you green money that first little black dot he took a bead on, that was the bitch of the bunch. First one is tough, no fuckin' foolin'. The second one … the second one ain't no fuckin' Mardis Gras either, but it's better than the first one 'cause you still feel the same thing, you know … except it's more diluted, y'know it's … it's better. I threw up on the first one, you believe that? Then the third one … the third one is easy, you level right off. It's no problem. Now … shit … now I do it just to watch their fuckin' expression change.

The Last Seduction [1994]

CLAY GREGORY: He won't hurt you. I need a New Yorker for that.

Shallow Grave [1994]

JULIET MILLER: I can't do it.

ALEX LAW: But Juliet, you're a doctor. You kill people every day.

Clockers [1995]

DET. ROCCO KLEIN [LOOKS AT VICTIM'S SPLATTERED HEAD]: The kid had brains.

COP: Must be his golf jacket—got eighteen holes.

Devil in a Blue Dress [1995]

RAYMOND "MOUSE" ALEXANDER: You just said don't shoot him, right?

EASY RAWLINS: That's right.

RAYMOUND "MOUSE" ALEXANDER: Well, I didn't. I just … choked him.

AK-47. The very best there is. When you absolutely, positively got to kill every motherfucker in the room. Accept no substitutes.

—ORDELL ROBBIE

Jackie Brown
1997

Heat [1995]

NEIL McCAULEY: Stay down. We want to hurt no one. We're here for the bank's money, not your money. Your money is insured by the federal government, you're not gonna lose a dime. Think of your families, don't risk your life. Don't try and be a hero.

Strange Days [1995]

LENNY NERO [GUY POINTS GUN IN HIS FACE]: Two million years of human evolution, that's the best idea you can come up with.

The Usual Suspects [1995]

MICHAEL McMANUS [AIMS THROUGH A SNIPER SCOPE]: Old McDonald had a farm, e-i, e-i-o. And on this farm he shot some guys. Ba-da-bip, ba-da-bing, bang-boom.

....

MICHAEL McMANUS: Oswald was a fag.

Blood and Wine [1996]

ALEX GATES: Well, Vic, at least you got to die in your own clothes. That's something.

Hard Eight [1996]

JOHN FINNEGAN: I'll fuck you up if you fuck with me. I know three types of Karate, OK? Jujitsu, Aikido, and regular Karate.

Cop Land [1997]

LT. MOE TILDEN: I didn't know they allowed classical music in Jersey.

....

GARY "FIGGSY" FIGGIS: I mean, H. G. Wells, he'd turn over in his grave to think at the start of the new millennium some Iranian guy …

BERTA: Armenian.

GARY "FIGGSY" FIGGIS: . . . some Armenian would be delivering a goat's head to the door of the woman that he loves.

RAY DONLAN: I always liked you, Murray. You just sweat too much.

L.A. Confidential [1997]

CAPT. DUDLEY SMITH: I admire you as a policeman, particularly your adherence to violence as a necessary adjunct to the job.

U Turn [1997]

BOBBY COOPER: Because you're a slimy bastard who'd have his wife killed to get his hands on some money.

JAKE McKENNA: What does that make you?

BOBBY COOPER: The slimy bastard that's gonna do it.

The Big Lebowski [1998]

WALTER SOBCHAK: You want a toe? I can get you a toe, believe me. There are ways, Dude. You don't wanna know about it, believe me.

THE DUDE: Yeah, but Walter . . .

WALTER SOBCHAK: Hell, I can get you a toe by three o'clock this afternoon—with nail polish.

WALTER SOBCHAK: Nihilists? Fuck me. I mean, say what you like about the tenets of National Socialism, Dude, at least it's an ethos.

And I guess that was your **accomplice** in the **woodchipper.**

—POLICE CHIEF
MARGE GUNDERSON

Fargo
1996

Are these the **Nazis**, Walter? —DONNY

No, Donny, these men are **nihilists**. There's nothing to be afraid of. —WALTER SOBCHAK

The Big Lebowski 1998

Clay Pigeons [1998]

LESTER LONG: It's all very simple, Clay. There are some people out there that need—need—killing.

....

LESTER LONG: So how they treating you? You doing OK back there?

CLAY BIDWELL: I'm charged with murder.

LESTER LONG: Only one count. Don't be such a fucking pussy all the time, please.

Following [1998]

THE BLONDE: Did you enjoy beating him up?

COBB: Of course.

Ronin [1998]

SPENCE: You ever kill anybody?

SAM: I hurt somebody's feelings once.

Twilight [1998]

HARRY ROSS: The one thing that you can count on if you're a private investigator is that, anytime a client says, "You don't need to carry a gun," that's when you ought to bring two.

Best Laid Plans [1999]

JIMMY: I got a sofa at home smarter than you.

....

BRYCE: You mean actually kill her, take her life?

NICK: No, the other sense of the word kill.

The Limey [1999]

JIM AVERY: How's it going, kid?

STACY: Not bad.

JIM AVERY: How'd you like to kill someone for me?

STACY: OK.

2001–2005

Heist [2001]

DON "PINKY" PINCUS: Never liked the Swiss. They make them little clocks, these two cocksuckers come out of them, these little hammers, hit each other on the head. What kind of sick mentality is that?

....

DON "PINKY" PINCUS: Go sell chocolate, you Heidi motherfuckers, go sell cuckoo clocks. We got your gold.

....

JOE MOORE: He ain't gonna shoot me?

FRAN MOORE: No.

JOE MOORE: Then he hadn't oughta point a gun at me. It's insincere.

Pueblo sin Suerte [2002]

CARLOS: If I cut out your tongue you would still be alive. That's your problem.

Ripley's Game [2002]

TOM RIPLEY: You know the most interesting thing about doing something terrible?

JONATHAN TREVANNY: What?

TOM RIPLEY: Often, after a few days, you can't even remember it.

....

TOM RIPLEY: Keep my watch, because if it breaks, I'll kill everyone on this train.

....

TOM RIPLEY: Your entire education comes from *Classic Car* magazine, and you dress like you're making a condom run for the mob.

....

TOM RIPLEY: Uh, do you want to tell me what you want, or do you want some truffling pig to find you dead somewhere in a month or two?

The Cooler [2003]

SHELLY KAPLOW [BEATS UP CORPORATE YUPPIE IN THE BATHROOM]**:** Now listen to me, you little Harvard turd. Lootz is all right, so he's walking out of here with everything he's got coming to him. And if you so much as touch one fucking hair on his fucking head, I'm gonna fucking wallpaper this fucking bathroom with your fucking ass, you understand me? Muted tones, isn't that what you said, huh? Huh? I can't hear you. Wait, wait a minute. There it is. Blended in, at a subsonic level, like some kind of mantra: "Pain, pain, pain."

Mystic River [2003]

JIMMY MARKUM [BEFORE HE KILLS DAVE BY THE RIVER]**:** We bury our sins here, Dave. We wash them clean.

Don't **threaten** me. I'm not the one wearing an earring.

—TOM RIPLEY

Ripley's Game 2002

Sin City [2005]

DWIGHT: Hi. I'm Shellie's new boyfriend and I'm out of my mind. You ever so much as talk to Shellie again, you even think her name, and I'll cut you in ways that'll make you useless to a woman.

JACKIE BOY: You're making a big mistake, man. A big mistake.

DWIGHT: Yeah. You made a big mistake yourself. You didn't flush. [PUSHES JACK-IE BOY'S HEAD INTO TOILET]

....

DWIGHT: She doesn't quite chop his head off. She makes a Pez dispenser out of him.

....

DWIGHT: Sure he's dead. Sure I'm just imagining that he's talking. None of that stops the bastard from being absolutely right.

....

DWIGHT: Miho. You're an angel. You're a saint. You're Mother Teresa. You're Elvis. You're God. And if you'd shown up ten minutes earlier, we'd still have Jackie Boy's head.

....

MARV: I love hit men. No matter what you do to them, you don't feel bad.

Eliminate me. Will that give you satisfaction, my son? Killing a helpless old fart. —CARDINAL ROARK

The killing, no. No satisfaction. Everything up to the killing will be a gas. —MARV

Sin City 2005

To me, *stealing's always been a lot like sex.* Two people who want the same thing: They get in a room, they talk about it. They start to plan. *It's kind of like flirting.* It's kind of like foreplay, 'cause the more they talk about it, the wetter they get. —CORKY

Bound 1996

CHAPTER FOUR

The Money and the Grubbing

1941–1950

The Maltese Falcon [1941]

SAM SPADE: We didn't exactly believe your story, Miss. O'Shaughnessy. We believed your $200.

....

SAM SPADE: I mean you paid us more than if you had been telling us the truth, and enough more to make it alright.

....

SAM SPADE: Haven't you tried to buy my loyalty with money and nothing else?

BRIGID O'SHAUGHNESSY: What else is there I can buy you with?

Laura [1944]

DET. LT. MARK McPHERSON: Nice little place you have here, Mr. Lydecker.

WALDO LYDECKER: It's lavish, but I call it home.

Murder, My Sweet [1944]

PHILIP MARLOWE: It was a nice little front yard. Cozy, OK for the average family. Only you'd need a compass to go to the mailbox. The house was alright, too, but it wasn't as big as Buckingham Palace.

Detour [1945]

AL ROBERTS: Money. You know what that is, it's the stuff you never have enough of. Little green things with George Washington's picture that men slave for, commit crimes for, die for. It's the stuff that has caused more trouble in the world than anything else we ever invented, simply because there's too little of it.

....

AL ROBERTS: A piece of paper crawling with germs.

Mildred Pierce [1945]

VEDA PIERCE: With this money I can get away from you.

MILDRED PIERCE: Veda.

VEDA PIERCE: From you and your chickens and your pies and your kitchens and everything that smells of grease. I can get away from this shack with its cheap furniture. And this town with its dollar days, its women who wear uniforms and its men who wear overalls.

....

VEDA PIERCE: You think that just because you've made a little money you can get a new hairdo and some expensive clothes and turn yourself into a lady. But you can't, because you'll never be anything but a common frump whose father lived over a grocery store and whose mother took in washing.

There's one good thing in being a **widow,** isn't there? You don't have to ask your husband for money.

—MRS. POETTER

Shadow of a Doubt
1943

It was like feeding time at the zoo. All you needed was money to start with and bicarbonate of soda to finish with.

—CAPT. WARREN "RIP" MURDOCK

Dead Reckoning 1947

The Spiral Staircase [1946]

PROFESSOR WARREN: What a pity my father didn't live to see me become strong, to see me dispose of the weak and imperfects of the world whom he detested. He would have admired me for what I am going to do.

Body and Soul [1947]

CHARLEY DAVIS: I take the beatings and you take the dough, like all the rest of them.

Brighton Rock [1947]

COLLEONI: Do you see the gold on them furnitures? Napoleon the third used to have this room with Eugenie.

PINKIE BROWN: Who was she?

COLLEONI: Oh, some foreign palone.

Brute Force [1947]

MUGSY: I got a favor to propose you.

GUARD: Don't ask me no favors. I can't be bribed, see? Besides, you ain't got enough dough to bribe me.

Lady in the Lake [1947]

ADRIENNE FROMSETT: Now what am I supposed to do, reform? Become poor but honest? On what corner would you like me to beat my tambourine?

....

ADRIENNE FROMSETT: I've been pushed around too much in this world. There's more than one Kingbsy on the Christmas tree Mr. Marlowe, and I'll shake one loose yet, don't you worry.

Nightmare Alley [1947]

MOLLY CARLISLE: Have you an answer for this question?

STANTON CARLISLE: Oh, I'm afraid not.

MOLLY CARLISLE: Why?

STANTON CARLISLE: Because that has to do with the stock market. A labyrinth whose eccentricities no mentalist of my acquaintance has ever been able to solve. As a matter of fact, I tried it two or three times myself and find that I can do much better at the race track.

Out of the Past [1947]

JEFF BAILEY/JEFF MARKHAM: I sell gasoline, I make a small profit. With that, I buy groceries. The grocer makes a profit. We call it earning a living. You may have heard of it somewhere.

Quai des Orfèvres [1947] aka *Jenny Lamour*

MARGUERITE CHAUFFORNIER MARTINEAU/JENNY LAMOUR: You're jealous of the rich. Well, I want my share of their dough. I'm all for royalty.

Ride the Pink Horse [1947]

FRANK HUGO: Small fry. All your life you waste time worrying about small fry things. About a job. About a two buck raise. About getting a pension.

....

FRANK HUGO: Guys like you work all their lives breaking their backs, trying to earn meat and potatoes. You end up borrowing enough money to buy a hole in the ground to get buried in. Then when you get a chance to make some real scratch, what do you do, mice like you and Shorty? You ask for peanuts.

Force of Evil [1948]

WALLY: What do you mean "gangsters"? It's business.

....

JOE MORSE: I will tell you, Doris, how the boom was on and I could feel money spread all over the city like air. Like perfume from those flowers I gave you. I could breathe the smell of money.

Pitfall [1948]

TOMMY FORBES: Is there anything you want me to do today, Dad?

JOHN FORBES: Yeah. Until my rich uncle dies, quit growing.

Raw Deal [1948]

JOSEPH EMMETT "JOE" SULLIVAN: I told you he had a cash register mind. Rings every time he opens his mouth.

Sleep, My Love [1948]

DAPHNE: We've got a lot—but we haven't got everything. I want what she's got. All of it. I want her house, her name, her man. And I want them now. Tonight.

The Street With No Name [1948]

ALEC STILES: Here. Buy yourself a closetful of clothes. I like my boys to look sharp.

Deadly Is the Female [1949] aka *Gun Crazy*

BART TARE: Two people dead, just so we can live without working.

ANNIE LAURIE STARR: Bart, I want things. A lot of things. Big things.

As they say, life begins with fifty Gs.

—JOSEPH EMMETT "JOE" SULLIVAN

Raw Deal
1948

The Money and the Grubbing

Abandoned [1949]

MORRIE THE BOOKIE: Why do you want to throw your money away on children? Play the races.

Too Late for Tears [1949]

ALAN PALMER: The money won't buy you anything. It'll only make you miserable and unhappy.

JANE PALMER: Let me be the judge of that.

The Asphalt Jungle [1950]

DOC: One way or another we all work for our vice.

Kiss Tomorrow Goodbye [1950]

HOLIDAY CARLETON: He's too smart for you.

RALPH COTTER: Oh no, he stopped being smart when he took my money.

The Underworld Story [1950]

MIKE REESE: I never asked you for a nickel, baby, did I?

FEMALE REPORTER: You wouldn't have gotten it. You were never worth that much.

....

JERRY BLAKE: Lakeville—you know, that's a good spot for you. A cemetery surrounded by bluebloods. One of those ivy-covered towns, shiny on top. You know what's underneath the ivy, Mike? Little crawling things. You should feel right at home there.

....

DIST. ATTORNEY RALPH MUNSEY: Take it easy, Reese. Things are tough all over. Pretty soon a man won't be able to sell his own mother.

Good-bye, angel.
And don't forget to change your will.
You'd hate yourself
on your little pink cloud
if you accidentally
left anything to me.

—HOWARD FRAZER

The Man Who Cheated Himself
1951

Money isn't dirty, just people.

—LONA McLANE

Pushover 1954

Sunset Boulevard [1950]

JOE GILLIS: Would you believe me if I told you I stayed with a sick friend?

ARTIE GREEN: Someone in the formal set, no doubt, with a ten-carat kidney stone.

....

NORMA DESMOND: Shut up. I'm rich. I'm richer than all this new Hollywood trash. Huh-huh. I've got a million dollars.

JOE GILLIS: Keep it.

NORMA DESMOND: Own three blocks down-town. I've got oil in Bakersfield. Pumping, pumping, pumping.

1951–1960

His Kind of Woman [1951]

DAN MILNER: When I have nothing to do at night and can't think, I always iron my money.

LENORE BRENT/LIZ BRADY: What do you press when you're broke?

DAN MILNER: When I'm broke, I press my pants.

The Mob [1951]

SMOOTHIE: Ten thousand dollars isn't ex-actly starvation wages.

DET. JOHNNY DAMICO: No, you can buy a lot of smiles with it.

It's a Bitter Little World

The Man Who Cheated Himself [1951]

LT. ED CULLEN: What's a million or two between friends?

The Narrow Margin [1952]

DET. SGT. WALTER BROWN: You're a pretty good judge of crooks, Mrs. Neall. The only place you slip up is with cops. I turned the deal down.

MRS. NEALL: Then you're a bigger idiot than I thought. When are you going to get it through your square head that this is big business? And we're right in the middle.

DET. SGT. WALTER BROWN: Meaning you'd like to sell out?

MRS. NEALL: With pleasure and profit, and so would you. What are the odds if we don't? I sing my song for the grand jury, and spend the rest of my life dodging bullets—if I'm lucky—while you grow old and gray on the police force. Oh, wake up, Brown. This train's headed straight for the cemetery. But there's another one coming along, a gravy train. Let's get on it.

DET. SGT. WALTER BROWN: Mrs. Neall, I'd like to give you the same answer I gave that hood—but it would mean stepping on your face.

....

JOSEPH KEMP: All right copper, I'm not in this alone, but you are. You're just one guy buckin' a big company, don't matter if you beat my brains out or not—we're in business for keeps.

Pickup on South Street [1953]

"MOE" WILLIAMS: Every extra buck has a meaning all its own.

....

"MOE" WILLIAMS: I have to go on making a living so I can die.

....

SKIP MCCOY: So you're a Red, who cares? Your money's as good as anybody else's.

Pushover [1954]

DET. RICK McALLISTER: Money's nice, but it doesn't make the world go round.

DET. PAUL SHERIDAN: Don't it?

Du Rififi Chez les Hommes [1955] aka *Rififi*

MARIO FARRATI [OGLES THE TAKE FROM A ROBBERY]: Now Ida and me can try out beds in all the chic hotels.

....

NEWSPAPER VENDOR: Read all about it. Biggest take since the Sabine women.

The Killing [1956]

GEORGE PEATTY: It would make a difference, wouldn't it? If I had money, I mean.

SHERRY PEATTY: How would you define money, George? If thinking about giving me your collection of Roosevelt dimes ...

GEORGE PEATTY: I'm gonna have it, Sherry. Hundreds of thousands, maybe a million.

SHERRY PEATTY: Of course you are darling. Did you put the right address on the envelope when you sent it to the North Pole?

Sweet Smell of Success [1957]

SIDNEY FALCO: To tell you the truth, I never thought I'd make a killing off some guy's integrity.

J.J. HUNSECKER: I'd hate to take a bite outta you. You're a cookie full of arsenic.

....

SIDNEY FALCO: In brief, from now on the best of everything is good enough for me.

....

JIMMY: It's a dirty job, but I pay clean money for it.

Nowhere to Go [1958]

PAUL GREGORY: Look, Vic, I haven't seen that money for a long time. We'll want to be left alone together,

Odds Against Tomorrow [1959]

EARL SLATER: I'm off to make my fortune.

Like the man said, can MONEY buy happiness?

—VINCENT RAPALLO

Killer's Kiss 1955

What's that? —MARTY AUGUSTINE

A picture of James Madison. —PHILIP MARLOWE

It's a five-thousand-dollar bill.
—MARTY AUGUSTINE

I know. —PHILIP MARLOWE

Where'd you get this? —MARTY AUGUSTINE

A box of crackerjacks,
came as a prize. —PHILIP MARLOWE

The Long Goodbye 1973

LORRY: Ah … what kind of a fortune?

EARL SLATER: Just one of those … fortune fortunes.

1961–1970

Underworld, U.S.A. [1961]

SANDY: Have you got anything in mind by way of a job?

TOLLY DEVLIN: A job?

SANDY: Yeah it's a word, meaning work.

In Cold Blood [1967]

DICK HICKOCK: Everybody steals something some time. It's the national pastime, baby.

....

DICK HICKOCK: I don't know gold dust from diarrhea.

1971–1980

Across 110th Street [1972]

CAPT. FRANK MATTELLI: I only took gambling money.

DOC JOHNSON: Yeah, yeah, they all say that. No. No, you don't take whoring money. You don't take dirty junkie money. You only take nice clean numbers money. Where do you think it comes from, them envelopes? Dirty money or clean money, it's all the same.

That jerk Karl Marx said **opium** was the religion of the people. I got news for him. It's **money.**

—FLO

The Killing of a Chinese Bookie 1976

The Long Goodbye [1973]

MARTY AUGUSTINE: Let me tell you something else. It's a minor crime, to kill your wife. The major crime is that he stole my money. Your friend stole my money, and the penalty for that is capital punishment.

99 and 44/100% Dead [1974]

BIG EDDIE: But you work for me, and I can give you all the more of everything that you can cram inside your brain, stick under your skin, pour into your guts, or wrap your legs around.

Chinatown [1974]

JAKE GITTES: No, I just want to know what you're worth. Over $10 million?

NOAH CROSS: Oh my, yes.

JAKE GITTES: Why are you doing it? How much better can you eat? What can you buy that you can't already afford?

NOAH CROSS: The future, Mr. Gitts [sic], the future.

1981–1990

Thief [1981]

FRANK: I wear $150 slacks. I wear silk shirts. I wear $800 suits. I wear a gold watch. I wear a perfect D, flawless three-carat ring. I change cars like other guys change their fucking shoes. I'm a thief.

Blood Simple [1984]

LOREN VISSER: In Russia they make only fifty cents a day.

52 Pick-Up [1986]

ALAN RAIMY: Like a lot of people who make a lot of money, you don't seem to have any.

Kill Me Again [1989]

FAY FORRESTER: I'll pay you $10,000. Half now, the other half after I'm dead.

Miller's Crossing [1990]

JOHNNY CASPAR: It's getting so a businessman can't expect no return from a fixed fight.

....

JOHNNY CASPAR: For a good return you gotta go betting on chance and then, you're back with anarchy. Right back in the jungle.

1991–2000

Romeo Is Bleeding [1993]

JACK GRIMALDI: A quarter goes into a phone booth and sixty-five grand comes out. Could you ask for better odds at Vegas?

....

MONA DEMARKOV: How'd you like to become a rich man, Sergeant?

JACK GRIMALDI: Well, I already got my health.

Blood and Wine [1996]

VICTOR SPANSKY: The interesting thing about rich people is, they're so cheap. They'll spend $1.3 million on a necklace, diamonds the size of chocolates, then they'll lock it in a tin box from Sears.

Fargo [1996]

POLICE CHIEF MARGE GUNDERSON: There's more to life than a little money, ya know. Doncha know that? And here ya are. And it's a beautiful day.

The Spanish Prisoner [1997]

GEORGE LANG: Fella said we must never forget that we are human. And as humans, we must dream, and when we dream, we dream of money.

A Simple Plan [1998]

HANK MITCHELL: You work for the American dream. You don't steal it.

....

HANK MITCHELL: We can't say this isn't stealing anymore.

SARAH MITCHELL: Well, Hank, it's always been stealing. We just didn't know who we were stealing from.

....

SARAH MITCHELL: What about me? Spending the rest of my life eight hours a day with a fake smile plastered on my face checking out books and then coming home to cook dinner for you, the same meals over and over again, whatever the week's coupons will allow, only going out to restaurants for special occasions, birthdays or anniversaries and even then having to watch what we order, skipping the appetizer, coming home for dessert. You think that's going to make me happy?

Best Laid Plans [1999]

BAD ASS DUDE: Have you read Adam Smith's *An Inquiry into the Wealth and Causes of the Wealth of Nations*? In it the man addresses the two simple laws of the market. First law: self-interest. It is not through the benevolence of the butcher, the brewer, the fucking baker that we expect our dinner. But through their self-interest. I don't sell junk because I feel a civic duty, I do it out of ...?

NICK: Self-interest.

BAD ASS DUDE: Second law: competition. Only under the check of competition is a man's self-interest regulated from ruthlessness. I don't charge a C-note a pop because I think some other dude's gonna underprice me. I don't overcharge because what suppresses me ...?

NICK: Competition.

BAD ASS DUDE: Consequently, man's motivations of ...

NICK: Self interest ...

BAD ASS DUDE: ... are transmuted by ...

NICK: Competition ...

BAD ASS DUDE: ... to yield social harmony. You, motherfucker, have fucked with the laws of the market. You have fucked with competition. You have deregulated the self-interests of some other dope-peddling fuck. You done fucked up harmony. You must un-fuck it. This is all simple economics.

The Way of the Gun [2000]

PARKER: Now the longest distance between two points is a kidnapper and his money.

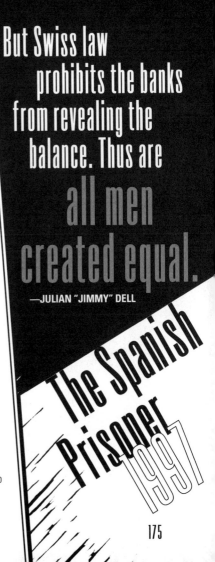

But Swiss law prohibits the banks from revealing the balance. Thus are all men created equal.

—JULIAN "JIMMY" DELL

The Spanish Prisoner 1997

Money is what you take to the grocery store. It's what you get out of an ATM. Fifteen million dollars is not money. It's a motive with a universal adapter on it.

—JOE SARNO

The Way of the Gun
2000

2001-2005

Heist [2001]

JOE MOORE [AFTER PUSHCART VENDOR GIVES HIM CHANGE BACK]: Makes the world go round.

BOBBY "BOB" BLANE: What's that?

JOE MOORE: Gold.

BOBBY "BOB" BLANE: Some people say love.

JOE MOORE: They're right too. It is love. Love of gold.

....

MICKEY BERGMAN: Everybody needs money. That's why they call it "money."

The Quiet American [2002]

THOMAS FOWLER: The smell, that's the first thing that hits you, promising everything in exchange for your soul.

Confidence [2003]

JAKE VIG: You can't just walk into the United States with a suitcase full of cash without invoking the words "cavity search."

Mystic River [2003]

DAVE BOYLE: Friend of mine says, the other day, he says, what the neighborhood needs is a good fuckin' crime wave to get property values back where they belong.

See, Mr. Gitts, most people never have to face the fact that, at the right time and the right place, they're capable of . . . anything.

—NOAH CROSS

Chinatown 1974

CHAPTER FIVE

The Life Lessons and the Death Wishes

1941–1950

I Wake Up Screaming [1941]

JILL LYNN: What's the good of living without hope?

POLICE INSP. ED CORNELL: It can be done.

The Maltese Falcon [1941]

SAM SPADE: Everybody has something to conceal.

....

KASPER GUTMAN: I distrust a man who says "when." If he's got to be careful not to drink too much, it's because he's not to be trusted when he does.

You know that stuff about pink elephants? That's the bunk. It's little animals. Little tiny turkeys in straw hats. Midget monkeys coming through the keyholes.

—"BIM" NOLAN

The Lost Weekend 1945

KASPER GUTMAN: I distrust a close-mouthed man. He generally picks the wrong time to talk and says the wrong things. Talking's something you can't do judiciously, unless you keep in practice. Now, sir, we'll talk if you like. I'll tell you right out, I'm a man who likes talking to a man who likes to talk.

SAM SPADE: When a man's partner is killed, he's supposed to do something about it.

DET. TOM POLHAUS [PICKS UP THE MALTESE FALCON]**:** Heavy. What is it?

SAM SPADE: The, uh, stuff that dreams are made of.

DET. TOM POLHAUS: Huh?

The Glass Key [1942]

JEFF: When I bite a steak, I like it to bite back at ya.

This Gun for Hire [1942]

WILLARD GATES: Don't you trust me?

PHILIP RAVEN: Who trusts anybody?

Shadow of a Doubt [1943]

UNCLE CHARLIE: What's the use of looking backward? What's the use of looking ahead? Today's the thing—that's my philosophy. Today.

ANN NEWTON: The ones that say they don't want anything always get more in the end.

UNCLE CHARLIE: Do you know the world is a foul sty? Do you know if you ripped the fronts off houses you'd find swine? The world's a hell. What does it matter what happens in it?

Detour [1945]

AL ROBERTS: That's life. Whichever way you turn, Fate sticks out a foot to trip you.

AL ROBERTS: Yes, Fate, or some mysterious force, can put the finger on you or me for no good reason at all.

The Lost Weekend [1945]

"BIM" NOLAN: Delirium is a disease of the night.

The Blue Dahlia [1946]

JOHNNY MORRISON: You oughta have more sense than to take chances with strangers like this.

JOYCE HARWOOD: It's funny, but practically all the people I know were strangers when I met them.

The Chase [1946]

CHUCK SCOTT: For me it was cheap hotels, cheap restaurants, cheap friends. All places are alike when you're broke, you know.

Crack-Up [1946]

GEORGE STEELE: Face to face with a painting, we shuffle our feet and apologize. We say "I don't know much about art, but I know what I like." Well, why apologize? If knowing what you like is a good enough way to pick out a wife or a house or a pair of shoes, what's wrong with applying the same rule to paintings?

The Killers [1946]

JAIL WARD DOCTOR: He's dead now, except he's breathing.

Strange Impersonation [1946]

NORA GOODRICH: Surely you must know some people in your own home town.

JANE KARASKI: They're all dead back there.

Body and Soul [1947]

QUINN: Still thinking about Ben, Charley? Everybody dies. Ben, Shorty, even you.

CHARLEY DAVIS: What's the point?

QUINN: No point. That's life.

....

QUINN: Everything is addition or subtraction. The rest is conversation.

....

ROBERTS: What makes you think you can get away with this?

CHARLEY DAVIS : What are you gonna do? Kill me? Everybody dies.

Brighton Rock [1947]

DALLOW: Never say die, boy.

PINKIE BROWN: You've got to say it sometime.

....

MOTHER SUPERIOR: You can't understand, nor I, nor anyone for that matter, the appalling strangeness of the mercy of God.

Brute Force [1947]

CALYPSO [SINGS]: Brandy's the very best drink in the world./If you drink enough your toes get curled.

Life's like a ball game. You gotta **take a swing** at whatever comes along before you wake up and find it's the ninth inning.
—VERA

Detour 1945

[WATCHES KATHIE PLAY ROULETTE]

That isn't the way to win. —JEFF BAILEY

Why not? —KATHIE MOFFAT

'Cause it isn't the way to win. —JEFF BAILEY

Is there a way to win? —KATHIE MOFFAT

There's a way to lose more slowly. —JEFF BAILEY

Out of the Past 1947

DR. WALTERS: Calypso, statistics show that if the level of alcohol in the blood exceeds one-half of one percent, the blood pressure is affected. A cerebral condition occurs and then—you're cockeyed. And maybe that's the way it should be.

JOE COLLINS: Everything's OK? What's OK? Nothing's OK. It never was and it never will be until we're out. Get that?

MUGGSY: Every day I have to take the chow to them guys down the drainpipe. I don't like the job. The air down there is very unsanitary.

GUARD: Don't breathe in, just breathe out.

JOE COLLINS: I don't care about everybody else.

GALLAGHER: That's cemetery talk.

JOE COLLINS: Why not, we're buried, ain't we? Only thing is, we ain't dead.

Dark Passage [1947]

DR. WALTER COLEY: There's no such thing as courage. There's only fear, the fear of getting hurt and the fear of dying. That's why human beings live so long.

The Lady From Shanghai [1947]

ARTHUR BANNISTER: You've been traveling around the world too much to find out anything about it.

MICHAEL O'HARA: Now, New York is not as big a city as it pretends to be.

MICHAEL O'HARA: I've always found it very sanitary to be broke.

ELSA "ROSALIE" BANNISTER: You need more than luck in Shanghai.

MICHAEL O'HARA: It's a bright, guilty world.

MICHAEL O'HARA: To begin with, living on a hook takes away your appetite. You have no taste for any pleasure at all but the one that's burnin' in you. But even without an appetite, I've heard it's quite amazing how much a fool like me can swallow.

ARTHUR BANNISTER: Yeah, Mike's quite a hero. Quite a tough guy.

SAILOR: Mister, there ain't no such thing.

ARTHUR BANNISTER: No such thing as a tough guy?

SAILOR: What's a tough guy?

ARTHUR BANNISTER: I don't know.

SAILOR: A guy with an edge ... [POINTS TO JUKE BOX]. What makes him sing better than me? [POINTS TO HIS THROAT] Something in here. What makes it loud? A microphone. That's his edge.

ARTHUR BANNISTER: Edge?

SAILOR: A gun or a knife, a nightstick or a razor, something the other guy ain 't got. Yeah, a little extra reach on a punch; a set of brass knuckles; a stripe on a sleeve; a badge that says cop on it. A rock in your hand. Or a bankroll in your pocket. That's an edge, brother. Without an edge, there ain't no tough guy.

MICHAEL O'HARA: Everybody is somebody's fool. The only way to stay out of trouble is to grow old, so I guess I'll concentrate on that. Maybe I'll live so long that I'll forget her. Maybe I'll die trying.

Out of the Past [1947]

KATHIE MOFFAT: Oh, Jeff, I don't want to die.

JEFF BAILEY/JEFF MARKHAM: Neither do I, baby, but if I have to, I'm going to be the one who dies last.

Ride the Pink Horse [1947]

PANCHO: There are lots of people gonna get lots of things but they don't.

PANCHO: The big drinks is more best.

Did you ever spend
ten nights in a
          Turkish bath
looking for a man?
Well, don't.

—DENNIS O'BRIEN

T-Men 1947

PANCHO: Knife is good. Is more easy to fix. I got knifed three times. When you're young, everybody sticks knife in you.

Force of Evil [1948]

JOE MORSE: A man could spend the rest of his life trying to remember what he shouldn't have said.

Key Largo [1948]

GAYE DAWN: Better to be a live coward than a dead hero.

FRANK McCLOUD: When your head says one thing and your whole life says another, your head always loses.

Sorry, Wrong Number [1948]

HENRY STEVENSON: You can't live on dreams forever. Waiting only weakens you and your dream. My motto is: "If you want something, get it now."

The Street With No Name [1948]

ALEC STILES: Dead men make bad witnesses.

Abandoned [1949]

MARK SITKO: If a baby didn't die, where else could he go?

CHARLIE: I know where they come from. I don't know where they go.

Beyond the Forest [1949]

ROSA MOLINE: If I don't get out of here, I'll just die. Living here is like waiting for the funeral to begin.

Border Incident [1949]

ZOPILOTE: What is cheaper than time, señor? Everybody has the same amount.

City Across the River [1949]

BENNY WILKES: Never slug a guy while wearing a good watch.

Knock on Any Door [1949]

SOCIAL WORKER: I hope it works out.

ANDREW MORTON: So do I, but there've been very few miracles since the thirteenth century.

SOCIAL WORKER: Oh, if I were as cynical as you, I'd hang myself.

ANDREW MORTON: I'd be too cynical to trust the rope.

Rope of Sand [1949]

TOADY: Consider the diamond itself for instance. Carbon, soot, chemically speaking. And yet the hardest of all matters. So hard, in fact, that whatever it touches must suffer: glass, steel, the human soul.

....

SUZANNE RENAUD/ANISENELETETTE DURINGEAUD: The German is brittle. The Frenchman cries l'amour. The American is hoping for the cavalry to come.

ARTHUR "FRED" MARTINGALE: And what do Englishmen do?

SUZANNE RENAUD/ANISENELETETTE DURINGEAUD: They pay.

The Third Man [1949]

HARRY LIME: Nobody thinks in terms of human beings. Governments don't. Why should we? They talk about the people and the proletariat. I talk about the suckers and the mugs. It's the same thing.

....

MAJ. CALLOWAY: Death's at the bottom of everything, Martins. Leave death to the professionals.

....

MAJ. CALLOWAY: Next time we'll have a foolproof coffin.

....

HARRY LIME: But the dead are happier dead. They don't miss much here, poor devils.

The Set-Up [1949]

BOXER: Told you he was a sucker for a left.

GUS: Ah, everybody's a sucker for something.

....

STOKER: Everybody makes book on something.

....

TINY: How many times I gotta say it? There's no percentage in smartenin' up a chump.

....

STOKER: Well, that's the way it is. You're a fighter, you gotta fight.

White Heat [1949]

CODY JARRETT: Made it, Ma. Top of the world.

Dial 1119 [1950]

CHUCKLES [ABOUT THE TV IN HIS BAR]**:** Fourteen hundred bucks installed, the guy charges me. Push-button picture control, reflected image, three-by-four-foot screen. What do I get on it? Wrasslers. Crumbs.

....

HARRISON: Don't belittle wrestlers, Chuckles. They merely illustrate the society in which we live. We're all wrestlers. Everybody beats each other's brains out.

Kiss Tomorrow Goodbye [1950]

JOE "JINX" RAYNOR: And I'll tell ya something else he ain't. He ain't to be trusted.

RALPH COTTER: Why should he be different?

In a Lonely Place [1950]

MILDRED ATKINSON: Before I started to go to work at Paul's, I used to think that actors made up their own lines.

Blemishes are hid by night and
every fault forgiven. The world
should live by night.

The dark draws people together.
They can feel the need for each other.

But the world gives the night to the sick,
keeps for itself daylight, and lets men look
into faces filled with fear and hatred.

—ANN SEBASTIAN

The Sleeping City 1950

DIXON STEELE: When they get to be big stars, they usually do.

....

DIXON STEELE: There's no sacrifice too great for a chance at immortality.

Sunset Boulevard [1950]

JOE GILLIS: Psychopaths sell like hotcakes.

1951–1960

Affair in Trinidad [1952]

MAX FABIAN: Veronica, some people are mellowed by drink. I suggest you have another.

....

DOMINQUE: No one can live on grief. Yesterday is yesterday, tomorrow is tomorrow.

CHRIS EMERY: You left out today.

DOMINQUE: Today is already yesterday.

Another Man's Poison [1952]

DR. HENDERSON: Out of evil cometh good. That is, occasionally.

Clash by Night [1952]

JOE DOYLE: Why didn't you come home before?

MAE DOYLE D'AMATO: Why didn't I go to China? Some things you do, some things you don't.

....

MAE DOYLE D'AMATO: Home is where you come when you run out of places.

The Narrow Margin [1952]

SAM JENNINGS: Nobody loves a fat man except his grocer and his tailor.

The Steel Trap [1952]

JIM OSBORNE: The difference between the honest and the dishonest is a debatable line. We're suckers if we don't try to cram as much happiness as possible in our brief time, no matter how. Everybody breaks the law.

The Glass Web [1953]

JIMMY NEWELL: Hey, Mom, Dad really wrote a swell show this week, didn't he? Two murders.

LOUISE NEWELL: Shhh, Jimmy. The commercial's the most important part of the show.

Niagara [1953]

GEORGE LOOMIS: Why should the Falls drag me down here at five o'clock in the morning? To show me how big they are and how small I am? To remind me they can get along without any help? All right, so they've proved it. But why not? They've had ten thousand years to get independent. What's so wonderful about that? I suppose I could too, only it might take a little more time.

Pickup on South Street [1953]

"MOE" WILLIAMS: If I was to be buried in Potter's field, it'd just about kill me.

Bad Day at Black Rock [1955]

RENO SMITH: I believe a man is as big as what'll make him mad.

You're dead, son. Get yourself buried.

—J.J. HUNSECKER

Sweet Smell of Success 1957

Politicians,
ugly buildings,
and whores
all get respectable
if they last long enough.

—NOAH CROSS

Chinatown 1974

The Big Combo [1955]

MR. BROWN: First is first and second is nobody.

Kiss Me Deadly [1955]

aka *Mickey Spillane's Kiss Me Deadly*

DR. SOBERIN: But as the world becomes more primitive, its treasures become more fabulous.

The Harder They Fall [1956]

NICK BENKO: you wait around long enough and sooner or later everything falls right in your lap.

EDDIE WILLIS: Like rotten apples.

Sweet Smell of Success [1957]

SIDNEY FALCO: Cat's in the bag and the bag's in the river.

....

J.J. HUNSECKER: My right hand hasn't seen my left hand in thirty years.

....

SIDNEY FALCO: Don't do anything I wouldn't do—and that gives you a lot of leeway.

Odds Against Tomorrow [1959]

JOHNNY INGRAM: I can't lose forever.
DAVE BURKE: You'd be surprised.

1961–1970

Blast of Silence [1961]

NARRATOR: You learn the hard way: They all hate the gun they hire.

NARRATOR: A killer who doesn't kill gets killed.

BIG RALPH: I usually don't like birthday parties. You know, I figure, like, it's bad luck. I mean, like, why tempt fate?

Mélodie en Sous-Sol [1963]

aka *Any Number Can Win*

CHARLES: In life there are no big things—just fatalities.

The Killers [1964]

CHARLIE STROM: You see, the only man that's not afraid to die is the man that's dead already.

1971–1980

Klute [1971]

BREE DANIELS: Don't feel bad about losing your virtue. I always knew you would. Everyone always does.

The Friends of Eddie Coyle [1973]

JACKIE BROWN: This life's hard, man, but it's harder if you're stupid.

Chinatown [1974]

NOAH CROSS: You may think you know what you're dealing with, but believe me, you don't.

TELEPHONE CALLER/IDA SESSIONS: Are you alone?

JAKE GITTES: Isn't everyone?

It's a Bitter Little World

LAWRENCE WALSH: Forget it, Jake. It's Chinatown.

Night Moves [1975]

NICK: For them that don't have football, there's always religion, right, Har?

The Killing of a Chinese Bookie [1976]

COSMO VITELLI: What's your truth is my falsehood. What's my falsehood is your truth, and vice-a-versa.

Who'll Stop the Rain [1978]

JOHN CONVERSE: I have no more cheap morals to draw from all this death.

1981–1990

Coup de Torchon [1981]
aka *Clean Slate*

LUCIEN CORDIER: Better the blind man who pisses out the window than the joker who told him it was a urinal. Know who the joker is? It's everybody.

LUCIEN CORDIER: Around here you've got to joke a little, or you'll wind up shooting yourself.

ROSE: They say there's only one death but a hundred ways of dying. I hope yours will be the worst.

The Life Lessons and the Death Wishes

Hey, you watch the Mickey Mouse Club? 'Cause you know what today ... today is? Today is Wednesday. It's Anything Can Happen Day.

—HARRY ANGEL

Angel Heart 1987

You can follow the action, which gets you good pictures. You can follow your instincts, which'll probably get you in trouble. Or, you can follow the money, which nine times out of ten will get you closer to the truth.

—JAKE GITTES

The Two Jakes 1990

Cutter's Way [1981]

ALEX CUTTER: Don't ever orgy with a pet monkey.

True Confessions [1981]

DET. TOM SPELLACY: Only the winner goes to dinner.

....

SEAMUS FARGO: Now, you show me a priest whose eyes twinkle all the time and I'll show you a moron.

Manhunter [1986]

HANNIBAL LECKTOR: Didn't you really feel so bad because killing him felt so good? And why shouldn't it feel good? Must feel good to God. He does it all the time.

House of Games [1987]

MIKE: What I'm talking about comes down to a more basic philosophical principle: Don't trust nobody.

....

MIKE: You can't bluff someone who's not paying attention.

The Grifters [1990]

SIMMS: The last modern thing I liked was the mini-skirt.

....

SIMMS: Sickness comes to us all, Mr. Dillon.

ROY DILLON: That's true, Mr. Simms.

SIMMS: We never know when, we never know why, we never know how. The only blessed thing we know is that it'll come at the most inconvenient, unexpected time, just when you've got tickets to the World Series. And that's the way the permanent waves.

Miller's Crossing [1990]

TOM REAGAN: Nobody knows anybody. Not that well.

TOM REAGAN: You don't hold elected office in this town. You run it because people think you run it. Once they stop thinking it, you stop running it.

LEO: Oh c'mon Tommy. You know I don't like to think.

TOM REAGAN: Yeah, but think about whether you should start.

JOHNNY CASPAR: If you can't trust a fix, what can you trust?

JOHNNY CASPAR: "Friends" is a mental state.

VERNA: Come on, Tom. You know me a little.

EDDIE DANE: You ever notice how the snappy dialog dries up once a guy starts soiling his union suit?

The Two Jakes [1990]

JAKE GITTES: Sometimes it's best to follow the piece that doesn't fit.

KHAN: Does that mean you are happy?

JAKE GITTES: Who can answer that question off the top of their head?

KHAN: Anyone who's happy.

JAKE GITTES: I don't want to live in the past, Khan, I just don't want to lose it.

JAKE GITTES: Memories are like that: as unpredictable as nitro and you never know what's going to set one off.

JAKE GITTES: Like the clues that keep you on the right track are never where you look for them. They fall out of the pocket of somebody else's suit you pick up at the cleaners. They're in the tune you can't stop humming that you never heard in your life. They're at the other end of the wrong number you dial in the middle of the night. The signs are in all of those old familiar places you only think you've never been before. But you get used to seeing them out of the corner of your eye. And you end up tripping over the ones that are right in front of you.

JAKE GITTES: You can't trust a guy who's never lost anything.

1991–2000

Dead Again [1991]

COZY CARLISLE: Someone's either a smoker or a non-smoker. There's no in-between. The trick is to find out which one you are, and be that.

MIKE CHURCH: Yeah, well, you know, I'm … I'm still trying to quit, so …

COZY CARLISLE: Don't tell me you're trying to quit. People who say they're trying to quit are basically pussies who cannot commit. Find out which one you are, and be that.

Romeo Is Bleeding [1993]

JACK GRIMALDI: You ever wonder what hell is like? Maybe it ain't the place you think. Fire and brimstone. Devil with horns poking you in the butt with a pitchfork? What's hell? The time you should have walked, but you didn't. That's hell.

JACK GRIMALDI: It's hard digging a grave when the guy it's for is staring straight at you.

True Romance [1993]

CLIFFORD WORLEY: You know, I don't believe you.

VINCENZO COCCOTTI: That's of minor importance. What is of major fucking importance is that I believe you.

Keaton always said, "I don't believe in God, but I'm afraid of him."

—VERBAL KINT

The Usual Suspects 1995

Smokey,
this is not 'Nam.
This is bowling.
There are rules.
—WALTER SOBCHAK

The Big Lebowski
1998

Shallow Grave [1994]

ALEX LAW: I need to die misunderstood.

Waga Jinsei Saiaku No Toki [1994]

aka *The Most Terrible Time in My Life*

YANG DEJIAN: Hai Ping, even dogs, you know, dream of becoming masters.

Strange Days [1995]

MAX PELTIER: You know how I know it's the end of the world, Lenny?

LENNY NERO: No, tell me.

MAX PELTIER: Because everything's already been done, you know. Every kind of music's been tried, every government's been tried, you know. Fuckin' hairstyle, fuckin' bubble gum flavors, breakfast cereal, every type of fucking. You know what I mean? What are we gonna do now, man? How we gonna make another thousand years, for Christ's sake? I'm telling you man, it's over. We used it all up.

....

LORNETTE "MACE" MASON: Memories are meant to fade, Lenny. They're designed that way for a reason.

The Underneath [1995]

MICHAEL CHAMBERS: There's what you want and there's what's good for you. Ah, they never meet.

The Usual Suspects [1995]

KOBAYASHI: One cannot be betrayed if one has no people.

Blood and Wine [1996]

VICTOR SPANSKY: Cremation is the civilized choice. Ashes straight to ashes. Skip the whole business of decay and worms. I worry enough about worms as it is.

Bound [1996]

VIOLET: We make our own choices, we pay our own prices.

Hard Eight [1996]

SYDNEY: You know the first thing they should've taught you at hooker school? You get the money up front.

Hit Me [1996]

LENNY ISH: This used to be a three-star hotel. Used to be a five-star country.

L.A. Confidential [1997]

CAPT. DUDLEY SMITH: Go back to Jersey, Sonny. This is the City of the Angels and you haven't got any wings.

....

CAPT. DUDLEY SMITH: Don't start tryin' to do the right thing, boy-o. You haven't the practice.

Lost Highway [1997]

FRED MADISON: I like to remember things my own way.

ED: What do you mean by that?

FRED MADISON: How I remembered them. Not necessarily the way they happened.

The Spanish Prisoner [1997]

GEORGE LANG: Somebody said, "Nobody going on a business trip would be missed if he didn't arrive."

....

GEORGE LANG: Worry is like interest paid in advance on a debt that never comes due.

Only three rules in life, Tom Welles. **One**, there's always a victim. And **two**, don't be it. —MAX CALIFORNIA

And Three? —TOM WELLES

I forgot **three**.

—MAX CALIFORNIA

8MM 1999

Doris wasn't big on divine worship. And I doubt if she believed in life everlasting. She'd most likely tell you that our reward is on this earth, and bingo is probably the extent of it.

—EDWARD "ED" CRANE

The Man Who Wasn't There 2001

U Turn [1997]

JAKE McKENNA: A man who's got no ethics is a free man.

....

JENNY: Do you like Patsy Cline? I just love her. How come I wonder she don't put out no more new records?

BOBBY COOPER: 'Cause she's dead.

JENNY: Oh … gee, that's sad. Don't that make you sad?

BOBBY COOPER: I've had time to get over it.

The Big Lebowski [1998]

JACKIE TREEHORN: You know, people forget that the brain is the biggest erogenous zone.

THE DUDE: On you maybe.

Ronin [1998]

VINCENT: Under the bridge by the river, how did you know it was an ambush?

SAM: Whenever there is any doubt, there is no doubt. That's the first thing they teach you.

VINCENT: Who taught you?

SAM: I don't remember. That's the second thing they teach you.

Rounders [1998]

MIKE McDERMOTT: Hey, how'd you know I was coming back?

LESTER "WORM" MURPHY: That's easy. Who's your favorite actor? Clint Eastwood. *The Outlaw Josey Wales,* man. *The Man With No Name.* He always doubled back for a friend.

MIKE McDERMOTT: If you can't spot the sucker in your first half hour at the table, then you are the sucker.

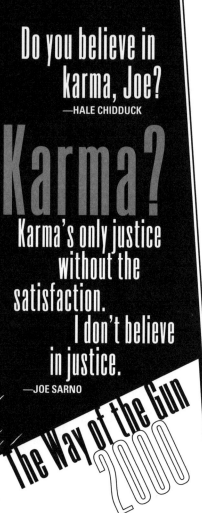

Do you believe in karma, Joe?
—HALE CHIDDUCK

Karma?

Karma's only justice without the satisfaction. I don't believe in justice.
—JOE SARNO

The Way of the Gun 2000

PROF. PETROVSKY: We can't run from who we are. Our destiny chooses us.

MIKE McDERMOTT: Like Papa Wallenda said, life is on the wire. The rest is just waiting.

A Simple Plan [1998]

JACOB MITCHELL [PONDERS CROWS]: Those things are always waitin' on something to die so they can eat it, right? What a weird job.

Twilight [1998]

HARRY ROSS: Ah, "used to be." We all "used to be."

8MM [1999]

MAX CALIFORNIA: Nobody knows what nobody knows, you know what I mean?

MAX CALIFORNIA: Pops, you dance with the devil, the devil don't change. The devil changes you.

The Way of the Gun [2000]

LONGBAUGH: You know what I want to tell God when I see him? I'm gonna tell him I was framed.

PARKER: Need is the ultimate monkey.

JOE SARNO: The only thing you can assume about a broken-down old man is that he is a survivor.

It's a Bitter Little World

LONGBAUGH [FACES THEIR DOOM]: What do you think?

PARKER: I think a plan is just a list of things that don't happen.

2001–2005

Heist [2001]

JOE MOORE: I wouldn't tie my shoes without a back-up plan.

JOE MOORE: Nobody can hear what you don't say.

Pueblo sin Suerte [2002]

JACK: Dumb times dumb is dumb doubled.

The Quiet American [2002]

THOMAS FOWLER: Even an opinion is a form of action.

THOMAS FOWLER: Morning, Hinh. Anything new?

HINH: Oh, corruption. Mendacity.

THOMAS FOWLER: I said anything new.

Ripley's Game [2002]

TOM RIPLEY: I don't worry about being caught, because I don't believe anyone is watching.

Wu Jian Dao [2002]

aka *Internal Affairs*

SAM: What millions died, that Caesar might be great?

The Cooler [2003]

SHELLY KAPLOW [RANTS ABOUT THE LAS VEGAS STRIP]: What, you mean that Disneyland mookfest out there? Huh? Come on, you know what that is? Huh? That's a fucking violation, is what that is. Something that used to be beautiful, used to have class, like a gorgeous high-priced hooker with an exclusive clientele. Then along comes that Steve Wynn cocksucker and knocks her up and put her in a fucking family way. Now she's nothing but a cheap, fat whore hiding behind too much fucking makeup. I look at her and see all her fucking stretch marks and it makes me want to cry because I remember the way she used to be. Am I right?

Mystic River [2003]

JIMMY MARKUM: I mean, the death part you do alone, but I coulda helped her with the dyin'. See what I'm sayin'?

Sin City [2005]

JOHN HARTIGAN: Get Senator Roark behind bars. Sure, and maybe after I pulled off that miracle, I'll go and punch out God.

....

SENATOR ROARK: Power don't come from a badge or a gun. Power comes from a lie. Lying big, getting the whole damn world to play along with you. Once you got everybody agreeing with what they know in their hearts ain't true, you got 'em by the balls.

It's a Bitter Little World

CHAPTER SIX

The Quotes That Dreams Are Made Of

Better to Be a Fake Somebody than a Real Nobody

"I'll tell you right out," Kasper Gutman says in *The Maltese Falcon*, "I'm a man who likes talking to a man who likes to talk." Gutman's talk was the same as Newton's gravity, Edison's electricity, or Thompson's submachine gun. He could have talked the Pope into converting to Satanism. And so could these writers, actors, and TV and Web personalities who supplied original noir quotes—exclusively for *It's a Bitter Little World*—and proved that, like Gutman, they can talk the talk with defibrillator dialog from movies that never were but should have been.

DEATH RIDES A UNICYCLE

BOBO: Listen Wheezie, this paint goes deep in my pores. It isn't a matter of quitting, it coats my soul.

WHEEZIE: Don't be ridiculous, I'll rub ya with some turpentine, toots.

—Harry Knowles, author of *Ain't It Cool?: Hollywood's Redheaded Stepchild Speaks Out* and *Ain't It Cool?: Kicking Hollywood's Butt* (www.aint-it-cool.com)

PUSSYCATS RULE!

CHUCKLES: I'm the big dog around here, little lady.

TURA: The difference between dogs and cats is, dogs do the ass-licking and pussycats do the ass-kicking.

—Tura Satana, star of Faster, *Pussycat! Kill! Kill!*

THE LAST FREE ELECTION IN AMERICA

GORE: These are desperate men and they will stop at nothing.

KERRY: Now you tell me.

—Gary Hart, former U.S. Senator

THE BIG LAYOVER

DUKE: I've got half a mind to tell you off, Kitty.

KITTY: You've got half a mind all right.

—Michael Musto, columnist for the *Village Voice* (www.villagevoice.com)

RIGHT TURN ON DEAD

ROCKY: She ate dinner like old people hump—slow and sloppy.

—Whit Watson, host and columnist for *Sun Sports* (www.sunsportstv.com)

BLONDE SATAN

SPIKE: I needed a dame like that in my life like a dog needs a diaper.

—Whit Watson, host and columnist for *Sun Sports* (www.sunsportstv.com)

DEAD MAN TALKING

LAUREN BACALL TO HUMPHREY BOGART: You know how to give someone the raspberry, don't you? Just put your tongue between your lips … and blow.

—John Wilson, founder (and head RAZZberry) of the Golden Raspberry "Razzie" Award (www.razzies.com)

LOVE AMONG THE PARANOID

MARIA: I want you to kiss me on the lips, hard and long, right now.

ARNOLD: What is this, a test?

—Paul Krassner, author of *Murder at the Conspiracy Convention: And Other American Absurdities* and *Magic Mushrooms and Other Highs: From Toad Slime to Ecstasy*

FILE IT UNDER MURDER

HARRIET, A SHAPELY LIBRARIAN: Do you need a pass to use the stacks?

DETECTIVE JIM MALLORY: I don't know … you tell me.

—John O'Dowd, author of *From the Glitter to the Gutter: The Rise and Fall of Hollywood Star Barbara Payton*

DARK FLOWER

MITCHELL: A wise man once said, "Every man and woman is a star."

VERONICA: I guess he never saw the people in the checkout line at Wal-Mart.

—Mark Frauenfelder, co-founder of *bOING bOING* magazine (www.boingboing.net)

The Quotes that Dreams are Made of

BELOW THE BELT

FLAKE: I'm tired, Buzz. Tired of this whole darn fight game.

BUZZ: Yeah? Doncha get enough sleep in the ring?

....

FLAKE: So what I'm 51? I can still dream. All it takes is one punch.

BUZZ: Kid, Kid! Don't you see? You'll always be one punch away from paradise.

—Tony Hendra, author of *Father Joe: The Man Who Saved My Soul* (www.tonyhendra.com)

FRUIT PUNCH

BUGS: So Bud nails me. It's a lucky punch. I'm lying there. The dumb palooka bends down and says: "'Scuse me Ma'am. I think you dropped your glove."

—Tony Hendra, author of *Father Joe: The Man Who Saved My Soul*
(www.tonyhendra.com)

THE DEVIL WORE LIPSTICK

DARLA: It's not like I chose this life, Dick. … This life chose me. Chose me like a gambler chooses a stacked deck, like a bum chooses a beat cop's billy club, like a dame chooses the guy who's never ever gonna treat her right. …

DICK: So what are you saying, Darla? That you can't get out? That you don't want to leave with me?

DARLA: That I don't want to get out, Dick. The grift is all I got.

—Ana Marie Cox, editor of *Wonkette* (www.wonkette.com)

THE LITTLE DEATH

SHE: Is that a snub-nosed .38 in your pocket, or are you glad to see me?

—Scott Rice, editor of *It Was a Dark and Stormy Night* and *Son of It Was a Dark and Stormy Night*, and organizer of the Bulwer-Lytton Fiction Contest (www.bulwer-lytton.com)

HOLLYWOOD 1-5-7-7

McGINLEY: Get this: I don't like you. I don't like mystery writers, especially ones who think cops are stupid or corrupt and make up some bright-boy private eye with a dimple in his chin and a smart mouth who's always showing up the lawmen. When did you ever solve anything besides a crossword puzzle?

—Alain Silver, co-editor of *Film Noir Reader* (www.filmnoirreader.com)

HOLLYWOOD 1-5-7-7

McGINLEY: How about you? Get a close look?

BARTENDER: Yeah. At his fist.

—Alain Silver, co-editor of *Film Noir Reader* (www.filmnoirreader.com)

HOLLYWOOD 1-5-7-7

BARTENDER: Don't mess with me, pal.

McGINLEY: Who are you kidding? You're not tough. The only thing you push around is a pencil.

—Alain Silver, co-editor of *Film Noir Reader* (www.filmnoirreader.com)

VIGORISH AND VITRIOL

TAYLOR: I told you, I'll get it, I swear. Somehow, I'll get it and pay you next week, I swear on my children.

BUTTERS: What is it about this situation you don't understand? I'll spell it out for you only because you're acting confused, like this situation is multiple choice, which it ain't. You took the man's money. That means he holds the freaking pink slip on your entire, miserable life … until you pay up. You savvy?

—Alan Rode, columnist for *Film Monthly* (www.filmmonthly.com)

THE BIG WARP

WES: I saw her through the frosted glass of my office door, a curvy silhouette that put Grable to shame. "It's open," I said, when she knocked. "That's funny," came the reply. "It looks closed to me." She was so beautiful, she made men stupid when she walked into the room. I know my IQ dropped like someone had just given it a Vulcan neck pinch.

—Wil Wheaton, writer and performer with the ACME Comedy Theater (www.wilwheaton.net)

THE THREE HATS

SULLY: Go easy on my gin—I've only got eight more bottles.

THELMA: Ah, quit yer bellyaching. The sooner this swill is gone, the better for the rest of your guests.

—Michael J. Nelson, author of *Mike Nelson's Death Rat!* (www.michaeljnelson.com)

THE DEVIL'S CHORD

SALLY: You come one step further and I'll tell Richard you tried to ravish me.

JOE: Go ahead—by the time he finished looking up the word I'll have flattened him.

—Michael J. Nelson, author of *Mike Nelson's Death Rat!* (www.michaeljnelson.com)

WAVE GOOD NIGHT, JAKE

PINKY: Should I go after him, Boss?

BUSTER: No. Go wait by the docks. That's where all the sewer rats end up eventually.

—Michael J. Nelson, author of *Mike Nelson's Death Rat!* (www.michaeljnelson.com)

THE OPAL OF MEERUT

MR. HOLLINGSFORD: I can't help noticing a certain snide tone in your voice, Mr. Winston.

MR. WINSTON: Good. Now pay attention to the snub nose in my hand, Mr. Hollingsford.

—Michael J. Nelson, author of *Mike Nelson's Death Rat!* (www.michaeljnelson.com)

THE LADY WORE BLACK

STELLA: I like a slow burn and a hot fuse.

DECKER: Is that why every guy you touch ends up looking like a spent bottle rocket right before I find his carcass?

—John Bloom (aka Joe Bob Briggs), author of *Profoundly Disturbing* and *The Joe Bob Report* (www.joebobbriggs.com)

SCRAMBLED

COP: I don't think we can put him back together for you, doll.

MOLL: I see. Thank-you, officer.

COP: Just one question. How did your husband come to have a great fall?

MOLL: You know how it is. I wanted an omelet.

—Regina Lynn, columnist for *Wired* magazine (www.wired.com/news and www.reginalynn.com), and Todd White

MAX HAMM FAIRY TALE DETECTIVE "NURSERY CRIMES"

MAX: Miss Muffet just sat there, crying. Normally I didn't take jobs that involved spiders. But I was a few curds shy of a way to pay the rent.

—Frank Cammuso, author of *Max Hamm, Fairy Tale Detective* (www.cammuso.com)

THE HEARTLESS ONE

BELLA: Don't you have no feelings for me, Rick? No sympathy?

RICK: Sympathy you want? Don't look for sympathy from me, you illiterate slut. Look in the dictionary. You'll find it between "sodomy" and "syphilis."

—Reinhold "Rey" Aman, editor of *Maledicta* journal (www.maledicta.org)

THE BIG HAPPY

EARL [VOICEOVER]: Ever done any hitchhiking? It's great. You meet the nicest people. I met this guy and he took me home to meet his family and then we had egg salad sandwiches. They gave me a fully paid train ticket for wherever I wanted to go.

Then I realized I didn't want to go anywhere. I work in the nicest nightclub. I'm a singer and I make so much money and all the customers are swell and I like them and they like me. I've been working there thirty-four years and the club is owned by this sweet old couple who are also big in the church.

I'm going to get some iced tea now, so refreshing. But that's just for a minute, because I'm aching to get out in the sunshine. It just makes me giggle. It makes my gal Kitty giggle too. Kitty's such a peach. She keeps hoping I'll give her a peck on the cheek, but oh no, not until we tie the knot, and even then. It's funny, I met this nice lady named Phyllis the other day. She was so upset that her husband was going to die. She said she thought that if she could cancel the insurance policy that he had taken out leaving her everything that maybe, just because she did that, he wouldn't die. I said sure, I'd help her. So we canceled the policy. Then we took all the money in her pocketbook and in my pockets and gave it to the little children, who were dreaming of candy bars.

—Toni Schlesinger, columnist for the *Village Voice* (www.villagevoice.com)

SLIM AND NONE

NICK: Can I have a word with you?

ZELDA: Yes, as long as it's "goodbye."

—Paul McFedries, author of *Word Spy* (www.wordspy.com)

NOW AND THEN

BIFF: I'm not the man I used to be.

STELLA: You never were.

—Paul McFedries, author of *Word Spy* (www.wordspy.com)

NIGHT OF THE VENETIAN BLINDS

SAM: I wouldn't trust that guy as far as I could throw him.

TOM: I wouldn't throw that guy as long as I could shoot him.

—David Rees, author of *Get Your War On* and *My New Fighting Technique Is Unstoppable* (www.mnftiu.cc)

RAISING CANE

MADELEINE: I find it hard to believe what they're saying about you and the oboe player.

MARK: Then don't believe it.

MADELEINE: You don't make it easy for your women, do you?

MARK: If you want easy, get a dog. No one forced you to sign up, Sugar.

MADELEINE: That's not what you said last night.

MARK: Last night was so long ago, I can't remember.

—Harley Hahn, author of *Harley Hahn's Internet Yellow Pages* (www.harley.com)

DARK PRECINCT

CAPT. ANDERSON: Nice collar, O'Brien, but couldn't you have fired a warning shot before plugging him three times in the back?

DET. LT. BARNEY O'BRIEN: Warning shots are for the jaywalkers.

—Mike Keaney, author of *Film Noir Guide: 745 Films of the Classic Era, 1940–1959* (http://members.cox.net/mike_keaney/)

THE LETTERS OF THE LAW

FRECKLES: I didn't mean it, baby.

MAX: Sure, doll … and I don't mean *this*.

FRECKLES: Oh, no! Not a Z on a triple letter score!

—Pat Sajak, host of *Wheel of Fortune* (www.patsajak.com)

THE BLONDE WORE BLACK

CRASH: Did it hurt me when she left? I'll say it hurt. Try pulling your nose hairs out with a pair of oversized, rusty pliers.

—Pat Sajak, host of *Wheel of Fortune* (www.patsajak.com)

THE MONEY HONEY

CUBBY: You're a dame, and I say you're a dame. A broad. A moll. A skirt. Old ball and chain.

LEXUS: Actually, I prefer "pre-op transgendered male-to-female."

—Slick Sharkey, contributor to the *Daily Probe* (www.dailyprobe.com) and to TopFive.com (www.topfive.com)

TRIPLE JEOPARDY

DRAVEN: What makes you think I'll take your case, follow you up into the canyon, and risk my life to find your uncle's lost silver mine?

STILLETTO: You're not smart enough to pass on a chance to be on a prime-time reality-TV show, are you?

—Slick Sharkey, contributor to the *Daily Probe* (www.dailyprobe.com) and to TopFive.com (www.topfive.com)

It's a Bitter Little World

The Best and the Bleakest

Happy Noir Year: 1946

The Big Sleep, Black Angel, The Blue Dahlia, The Chase, Crack-Up, The Dark Corner, Gilda, The Killers, Nocturne, Notorious, The Postman Always Rings Twice, The Spiral Staircase, The Stranger, The Strange Love of Martha Ivers

Happy Noir Year II: 1947

Body and Soul, Born to Kill, Brighton Rock, Brute Force, Crossfire, Dark Passage, Dead Reckoning, Kiss of Death, The Lady From Shanghai, Lady in the Lake, Nightmare Alley, Out of the Past, Pursued, Quai des Orfèvres, Railroaded!, Ride the Pink Horse, Singapore, T-Men

The Desert Noirs

Red Rock West
Ride the Pink Horse
U Turn

The Western Noirs

Broken Lance
The Badlanders
Pursued

The Science Fiction Noirs

Blade Runner
Strange Days
Dark City

The Bowling Noirs

The Big Lebowski
Cape Fear
Road House
Double Indemnity

The Sadists

TOMMY UDO, *Kiss of Death*
MR. BLONDE,
Reservoir Dogs
JEFF, *The Glass Key*
RICK COYLE, *Raw Deal*
POOH-BEAR,
The Salton Sea
BOBO JUSTUS, *The Grifters*
FRANK BOOTH, *Blue Velvet*
SAM WILDE, *Born to Kill*

The Amnesiacs

LEONARD SHELBY, *Memento*
JOHN MURDOCH, *Dark City*
BUZZ WANCHEK, *The Blue Dahlia*
JOHNNY McBRIDE, *The Long Wait*

The Chumps

CHRISTOPHER CROSS,
Scarlet Street
WALTER NEFF, *Double Indemnity*
JEFF BAILEY, *Out of the Past*
NED RACINE, *Body Heat*
JERRY LUNDEGAARD, *Fargo*
MIKE SWALE, *The Last Seduction*

The Black Widows

BRIDGET GREGORY,
The Last Seduction
PHYLLIS DIETRICHSON,
Double Indemnity
KATHIE MOFFAT, *Out of the Past*
VERA, *Detour*
LILY CARVER, *Kiss Me Deadly*
JANE PALMER, *Too Late for Tears*
MATTY WALKER, *Body Heat*
CATHERINE PETERSEN,
Black Widow

The Sluts

SHERRY PEATTY, *The Killing*
KITTY MARCH, *Scarlet Street*
GILDA, *Gilda*
VERNA JARRETT, *White Heat*

DEBBY MARSH, *The Big Heat*
IRENE NEVES, *Sudden Fear*
MATTY WALKER, *Body Heat*
MYRNA BOWERS,
   On Dangerous Ground
DODIE, *Appointment With Danger*

The Mr. Bigs

KEYSER SOZE, *The Usual Suspects*
NOAH CROSS, *Chinatown*
JOHNNY ROCCO, *Key Largo*
MIKE LAGANA, *The Big Heat*
JACKLAND AINSWORTH, *Railroaded!*
RICK COYLE, *Raw Deal*
FRANK HUGO, *Ride the Pink Horse*
MARSELLUS WALLACE, *Pulp Fiction*
HAROLD SHAND, *The Long Good Friday*

The Rich Bastards

NOAH CROSS, *Chinatown*
KEYSER SOZE, *The Usual Suspects*
GENERAL STERNWOOD, *The Big Sleep*
WALDO LYDECKER, *Laura*

The Scribblers

A.I. BEZZERIDES: *Kiss Me Deadly,*
   Thieves' Highway, On Dangerous
   Ground, They Drive by Night

**BILLY WILDER AND RAYMOND
   CHANDLER:** *Double Indemnity*

JONATHAN LATIMER: *The Glass Key,*
   They Won't Believe Me, The Big
   Clock, Night Has a Thousand Eyes

(co-writer), Nocturne (co-writer)

**BILLY WILDER, CHARLES BRACKETT,
   AND D.M. MARSHMAN, JR.:**
   Sunset Boulevard

**BILLY WILDER, WALTER NEWMAN,
   AND LESSER SAMUELS:**
   Ace in the Hole

**BILLY WILDER AND CHARLES BRACK-
   ETT:** *The Lost Weekend*

**ROBERT TOWNE AND ROMAN POLAN-
   SKI (UNCREDITED):** *Chinatown*

PAUL SCHRADER: *Taxi Driver*

ROBERT TOWNE: *The Two Jakes*

**CHARLES LEDERER, BEN HECHT AND
   ELEAZAR LIPSKY (UNCREDITED):**
   Kiss Of Death (1947)

**CHARLES LEDERER, BEN HECHT, AND
   JOAN HARRISON (UNCREDITED):**
   Ride the Pink Horse

JOHN DAHL AND DAVID W. WARFIELD:
   Kill Me Again

JOHN DAHL AND RICK DAHL:
   Red Rock West

The Monkey Music

CHINATOWN, *Jerry Goldsmith*
THE THIRD MAN, *Anton Karas*
   (uncredited)
TAXI DRIVER, *Bernard Herrmann*
DOUBLE INDEMNITY, *Miklós Rózsa*
THE ASPHALT JUNGLE, *Miklós Rózsa*
CRISS CROSS, *Miklós Rózsa*

ODDS AGAINST TOMORROW,
John Lewis
SWEET SMELL OF SUCCESS,
Elmer Bernstein

The Directors

ROBERT SIODMAK:
The Phantom Lady, The Strange Affair of Uncle Harry, The Spiral Staircase, The Killers, The Dark Mirror, The Suspect, Time Out of Mind, Cry of the City, Criss Cross, The File on Thelma Jordon

ALFRED HITCHCOCK:
Shadow of a Doubt, Notorious, Strangers on a Train, The Wrong Man, Vertigo

BILLY WILDER:
Double Indemnity, Sunset Boulevard, Ace in the Hole

ORSON WELLES:
The Stranger, The Lady From Shanghai, Touch of Evil

JOE LEWIS:
So Dark the Night, Deadly Is the Female, Desperate Search, Cry of the Hunted, The Big Combo

JULES DASSIN:
The Suspect, Thieves' Highway, Night and the City, The Naked City, Du Rififi Chez les Hommes, Brute Force

ANTHONY MANN:
Strange Impersonation, Desperate, Railroaded!, T-Men, He Walked By Night, Raw Deal

SAMUEL FULLER:
Pickup on South Street, The Naked Kiss, Underworld U.S.A.

ROBERT WISE:
Born to Kill, The Set-Up, Odds Against Tomorrow

ROBERT ALDRICH:
The Big Knife, Kiss Me Deadly

JOHN DAHL:
Kill Me Again, Red Rock West, The Last Seduction, Rounders

The Cinematography

CHINATOWN, *John A. Alonzo*
THE BIG COMBO, *John Alton*
BLADE RUNNER,
Jordan Cronenweth
TOUCH OF EVIL, *Russell Metty*
SWEET SMELL OF SUCCESS,
James Wong Howe
LAURA, *Lucien Ballard (uncredited) and Joseph LaShelle*
THE KILLING, *Lucien Ballard*
THE ASPHALT JUNGLE,
Harold Rosson
T-MEN, *John Alton*
HE WALKED BY NIGHT, *John Alton*
RAW DEAL, *John Alton*

The Books

The Art of Noir: The Posters and Graphics From the Classic Era of Film Noir.
Muller, Eddie. Woodstock, NY:
Overlook Press, 2002.

Dark City: The Lost World of Film Noir.
Muller, Eddie.1sts St. Martin's ed.
New York: St. Martin's Griffin, 1998.

The Dark Side of the Screen: Film Noir.
Hirsch, Foster. New York: Da Capo
Press, 1983.

Death on the Cheap: The Lost B Movies of Film Noir. Lyons, Arthur.
Cambridge: Da Capo Press, 2000.

Film Noir. Spicer, Andrew. New York:
Longman, 2002.

Film Noir: An Encyclopedic Reference to the American Style. Silver, Alain
and Elizabeth Ward, eds. 3rd. ed.
Woodstock, NY: Overlook Press,
1992.

Film Noir Guide: 745 Films of the Classic Era, 1940–1959. Keaney, Michael F.
Jefferson, NC: McFarland, 2003.

Film Noir Reader. Silver, Alain and
James Ursini, eds. 1st. Limelight ed.
New York: Limelight Editions, 2004.

Film Noir Reader 2. Silver, Alain
and James Ursini, eds. New York:
Limelight Editions, 2004.

Film Noir Reader 3: Interviews With Filmmakers of the Classic Noir Period.
Porfirio, Robert, Alain Silver, James
Ursini, eds. 1st. Limelight ed. New
York: Limelight Editions, 2001.

Film Noir Reader 4: The Crucial Films and Themes. Silver, Alain and James
Ursini, eds. 1st. Limelight ed. New
York: Limelight Editions, 2004.

The Noir Style. Silver, Alain and
James Ursini. Woodstock, NY:
Overlook Press, 1999.

101 Greatest Films of Mystery & Suspense. Penzler, Otto. New York:
ibooks: 2000.

**The Danger & Despair
Knitting Circle: A Resource
for Classic Film Noir**
www.noirfilm.com

Top-Rated Film Noir
www.imdb.com/chart

**Film Noir Current Month
TV Schedule**
www.tv-now.com/stars/
filmnoir.htm

Dark City: Film Noir and Fiction
www.eskimo.com/~noir

**What Is This Thing Called
Film Noir, Anyway?**
www.bighousefilm.com/
noir_intro.htm

**Mike Keaney's Film Noir
Home Page**
http://members.cox.net/
mike_keaney/guide.htm

The Film Noir Readers
http://members.aol.com/
alainsil/noir

Film Noir Films
www.filmsite.org/
filmnoir.html

**The Dark Room:
La Chambre Noir**
http://cinepad.com/filmnoir/
dark_room.htm

**High Heels on Wet
Pavement: Film Noir and
the Femme Fatale**
www.moderntimes.com/
palace/film_noir

Classic Noir Online
www.classicnoir.com

**Film Noir, Suspense, and
Classic Action Movies**
www.suspense-movies.com

Index